EMBRACING A DOCTRINE OF HOLINESS

Rob A. Fringer, series editor

EMBRACING A DOCTRINE OF HOLINESS

David B. McEwan • Rob A. Fringer

Global Nazarene Publications

ISBN 978-1-56344-950-5
rev2021-11-26

Global Nazarene Publication   Eurasia Regional Office
Lenexa, Kansas (USA)   Singapore

Copyright © 2021
David B. McEwan • Rob A. Fringer

DIGITAL PRINTING

TABLE OF CONTENTS

Introduction to *Frameworks for Lay Leadership* 6

Foreword 7

Chapter 1: Introduction.. 9

Chapter 2: The Biblical Understanding of Holiness................13

Chapter 3: The Meaning and Purpose of Life.........................21

Chapter 4: Love and Relationships are Primary.....................29

Chapter 5: Love Misdirected (The Problem)..........................35

Chapter 6: Love Renewed..43

Chapter 7: Love, Relationships, and Spiritual Formation.......65

Chapter 8: Conclusion..79

Appendix 83

Notes 85

Scripture tells us that believers are "a royal priesthood" (1 Peter 2:9). This means that all Christians, in one form or another, are called into places of ministry and leadership. Not only is this a great privilege, it is also a great responsibility. Men and women desiring to serve in church leadership in some capacity undergo basic training to assure that they understand the foundations of the Christian faith and of their Nazarene identity. This includes a deepening knowledge and appreciation of Scripture, theology, ministry, mission, history, and holiness. *Frameworks for Lay Leadership* is a series of six books designed to do just that—equip lay leaders for ministry in the Church, whether local, district, or general. These books have the greatest impact when they are read, processed, applied, and contextualised in partnership with a qualified mentor.

Welcome to this journey of transformation!

ENGAGING THE STORY OF GOD

EXPLORING A WESLEYAN THEOLOGY

EMBODYING A THEOLOGY OF MINISTRY AND LEADERSHIP

ENTERING THE MISSION OF GOD

EXPRESSING A NAZARENE IDENTITY

EMBRACING A DOCTRINE OF HOLINESS

FOREWORD

Rising from the need for an equipped laity to serve alongside the clergy of the districts of the Church of the Nazarene, the *Frameworks for Lay Leadership* series provides laypersons with extra tools to do the work of ministry. This series of six books for the development of lay leadership and the equipping of the Church for the work of ministry was written by gifted practitioners using easy-to-read language to address six areas of critical importance to the Church of the Nazarene.

Each volume addresses a subject area that clearly distinguishes the way Nazarenes should understand their place in the landscape of Christianity. While the volumes are intentionally concise for the busy leader, each contributor skilfully and comprehensively addresses their subject area, digging deep into related concepts to reveal the beauty of those concepts in simple and actionable language. Whether read individually or as a set, readers will lay down each volume with a deeper appreciation of who we are as Nazarenes, gain a clearer understanding of what we believe, and have a practical guide of how we should live, serve, and lead as children of God.

The series expresses a firm commitment to the mission of the Church of the Nazarene, "to make Christlike disciples in the nations". It enhances our understanding that the equipping, empowering, and engaging of the entire Church as the priesthood of all believers is an integral part of that mission. The *Frameworks for Lay Leadership* series serves as a practical vehicle that I highly recommend for adoption by district and local leadership.

The *Manual of the Church of the Nazarene* recognises that all believers are called to minister to all people (paragraph 500). It specifically provides for qualified lay ministers to serve in ministerial leadership under the supervision of a pastor and church board or a district superintendent and District Advisory Board (paragraphs 503-503.9). Bearing this in mind, *Frameworks* is designed to guide lay persons through a validated course of study to safeguard theological coherence and missional integrity as they engage in the leadership of ministries bearing the name Church of the Nazarene. Upon completion of these six books under the guidance of an ordained Nazarene minister, a certificate of lay ministry may be issued by a local church board or a District Advisory Board.

Dr Rob Fringer in his capacity as general editor of the series has my high commendation for bringing together this gifted team of contributors, and for guiding them through the development of each volume of the series. My sincere appreciation is also extended to each of the contributors for making time in the midst of busy schedules to develop this excellent resource that is already being used widely across the denomination.

Mark Louw
Director, Asia Pacific Region
Church of the Nazarene

CHAPTER 1

INTRODUCTION

The history of the Church gives us many models of what faithfulness to Christ and his people entails. It shows that a belief in entire sanctification (the "moment" when the heart is filled with God's love and sin is expelled) and an understanding of Christian perfection (perfect love and Christlikeness) have been present from the beginning. Although they have not always been kept connected, entire sanctification and Christian perfection are integral parts of a biblical doctrine of holiness. Their roots go back into both the Old and New Testaments and can be traced back to every age of Church history. The writings of the Church Fathers in the first five centuries and the great medieval theologians emphasise the place of perfect love and the work of the Holy Spirit. While the two great Protestant reformers, Martin Luther and John Calvin, believed in holy living, they focused on justification by faith alone and grace alone, rejecting the notion that we could be delivered from sin in this life. It is with the life and ministry of John Wesley, the key founder and early leader of Methodism, that the importance of entire sanctification and Christian perfection in the Christian journey were re-emphasised. Likewise, he clearly taught how Christian perfection was to be experienced in this life.

A doctrine of holiness becomes fundamental in Methodism and is the stated reason for its existence as a denomination. Wesley said it was the "grand [deposit] which God has lodged with the people called Methodists; and for the sake of propagating this chiefly, he appeared to have raised us up."[1] All the churches that trace their roots back to Wesley and the original Methodists (including the Church of the Nazarene) continue to believe in holiness of heart and life, although it is sometimes overlooked in practice. The revivals in the United States of America and the United Kingdom in the 19th century emphasised this doctrine. By the end of that century, several Holiness denominations and interdenominational movements formed. These groups saw their particular ministry as refocusing attention on both the doctrine and the experience of holiness (see the companion book in the series, *Expressing a Nazarene Identity*,[2] for more details).

In recent years, holiness has re-emerged as a crucial topic among many Christians who desire a deeper relationship with God and a genuinely transformed life that is able to make a difference in society. Our spiritual life is much more than a private affair between "Jesus and me"; it involves the whole Christian community. When we seek to understand holiness, we often turn to a book on doctrine. Many such books have a common presentation that revolves around definitions, biblical background, historical development, followed by a systematic presentation of the doctrine tied to important terms. It can become just another doctrine to be examined or debated rather than a relationship to be enjoyed, a life to be lived.

In the past, many churches within the Wesleyan-Holiness tradition focused on the defense of their understanding of holiness against detractors within the broader church, rather than promoting their understanding to the wider community as a way of life that is genuinely biblical and true to the revelation of Jesus Christ. Furthermore, sometimes our explanations have been full of religious terminology that no longer connects with the people of our church or community.

For many younger people or those new to our church, holiness seems to emphasise correct behaviour, a list of things we do not do and places we do not go, as if holiness is all about fulfilling a set of duties. In some settings, "holiness people" speak about it as a doctrinal understanding that must be mastered and then taught to others to convince them of our position. In other settings, holiness is all about embracing our inner, spiritual life and rejecting our physical appetites and desires. Too often, our arguments have centred on trying to make the Christian life either fit in with our culture or explain why we totally reject the culture.

Such notions of being holy are either unappealing or feel out of reach for many Christians. This assessment is not limited to our day and age. John Wesley also held this conviction early in his Christian ministry. His first surviving sermon (1725) paints a picture of the Christian life as one of suffering, misery, and failure.[3] His journey from that point would bring a total change of heart and mind. His study of church history and Christian doctrine did not lead to his transformation. Instead, it was a deep longing for an authentic Christian life that was both profoundly and personally satisfying that paved the way for his heart's change. His personal transformation contributed to the transformation of individuals and communities throughout the whole world. We all relate to this desire of Wesley, and it is this same conviction that lies at the heart of the Church of the Nazarene and our message of heart holiness.

We need to keep in mind that in our communities, and in the church, there is a variety of cultures, a wide range of experiences and ways of understanding, as well as a diversity of culturally influenced traditions. The challenge we face is to maintain unity and simultaneously recognise and celebrate diversity. Unity does not equal uniformity. Different aspects of the doctrine of holiness will connect with different people. Likewise, the various people and cultures in our church will identify with one or more of the different theological models of holiness. Yet, in all this rich diversity, we must not lose sight of the foundational models and accounts found in Scripture that require us to engage with all aspects of the doctrine and not just our favourite elements and descriptions.

This short book assumes a knowledge of the companion book in the series, *Exploring a Wesleyan Theology*,[4] and therefore will not retrace much of the core theological understanding of the doctrine of salvation. The layout in this book offers firstly a brief overview of the biblical understanding of the doctrine of holiness. We will then examine what it means to be created in God's image and to show how love and relationships are at the very heart of our existence. We then consider how our love is misdirected, focused on a selfish enjoyment of God's creation rather than an authentic love for God. By God's grace alone, our love can be purified, and rightly focused on God and then the neighbour and God's creation. Finally, we consider how habits of love are both formed and strengthened, so that we might truly reflect the life of Christ in this present existence.

QUESTIONS FOR REFLECTION

1. Why is the doctrine of holiness so important for our life in Christ?

2. In your culture, what are some of the ways you talk about holiness? What images do you use most often? How helpful are they when talking with new Christians in your church?

3. What are you hoping to learn from reading this book?

CHAPTER 2

THE BIBLICAL UNDERSTANDING OF HOLINESS

The starting point for any consideration of the doctrine of holiness must be the Bible (see the companion book in the series: *Engaging the Story of God*[5]). In Scripture, holiness is connected to the triune God (Father, Son, and Holy Spirit), and it is fundamental to our understanding of this God.[6] As the people of Israel proclaimed: "Who is like you, O Lord, among the gods? Who is like you, majestic in holiness, awesome in splendor, doing wonders?" (Exodus 15:11). Scripture makes multiple references to God's "holy name" (for example, Leviticus 22:32; Psalm 145:21; Isaiah 29:23; Ezekiel 36:21), and it posits that God's holiness extends throughout his creation—"Holy, holy, holy is the Lord of hosts; the whole earth is full of his glory"[7] (Isaiah 6:3). This God is holy and creates humanity in his image.

THE IMAGO DEI

The term *imago dei* (which is the Latin phrase for "image of God") is a significant biblical concept first introduced in the creation story of Genesis 1.

"Then God said, "Let us make humankind in our image, according to our likeness." ... So God created humankind in his image in the image of God he created them; male and female he created them" (Genesis 1:26-27).

There is much debate concerning what exactly this "image" and "likeness" entails, but we know that holiness is an important aspect of it. This is clearly articulated in Leviticus 19:2 when God says to the people, "You shall be holy, for I the Lord your God am holy." In this way, we can say that we have been created to be holy. While the imago dei may have been diminished as a result of sin and the Fall, the work of Christ beckons us back and enables us to reflect God's holiness once again. As the apostle Paul reminds us, we are being renewed in the image of our creator (Colossians 3:10), and "are being transformed into the same image from one degree of glory to another" (2 Corinthians 3:18).

Nevertheless, the potential holiness of any created person, place, or thing is always derivative.[8] That is to say, they are made holy based on their relationship to God or with God. This is made abundantly clear in the Old Testament. Things are made holy based on their proximity to God. For example, the tabernacle and all its various furnishings, especially the ark (Exodus 35–40), were holy because the tabernacle (and later the Temple) was God's earthly dwelling place. That is to say, the Temple was in close proximity to God. This holiness extended to Jerusalem (Isaiah 52:1) and ultimately to the whole land of Judah and Israel (Psalm 114:2). Similarly, any place where God revealed Godself became holy (Exodus 3:5; Deuteronomy 23:14). People could also be made holy by being set apart and consecrated to God. This was the case with the priests and Levites[9] (Leviticus 21; Numbers 3:5-13; 2 Chronicles 23:6), prophets (2 Kings 4:9; Jeremiah 1:5), those who took the Nazirite vow (Numbers 6:1-21), and ultimately the whole people of Israel (Deuteronomy 7:6; 14:2). Holy things included the various sacrificial offerings dedicated to God (Leviticus 1–7), as well as money, property, and even certain times, especially the Sabbath and the Day of Atonement.

An extreme form of dedication, often called "the ban" (in Hebrew, hērem), was reserved for objects and people that were seen as unredeemable (Leviticus 27:28-29). Thus, they were "dedicated" to God through total annihilation, which was usually connected to the concept of "holy war"[10] (for example, Deuteronomy 7:1-6, 17-26; Joshua 6:17-18; 1 Samuel 15:1-3). While unsettling to most modern readers, the concept was part of many ancient Near East cultures. For Israel, the dedication of war and its spoils to God was ultimately a form of worship, and it was believed to be God's "devouring fire" that consumed Israel's enemies (Deuteronomy 9:3).

THE LANGUAGE OF HOLINESS & SANCTIFICATION

The Hebrew root *qdš* and its cognates denote holiness or sanctification in the Old Testament and the Greek word *hagios* and its cognates in the New Testament. These words are very difficult to define. Since holiness is intrinsically tied to God, it could be described as "god-ness", a supernatural, transcendent otherness that ultimately belongs to God alone. As such, many have defined holiness in terms of "separation from" worldly people, places, and things. Nevertheless, God's actions in Scripture point to a more present and near God who continues to dwell among God's creation and desires a relationship with humanity. While there are clear examples of God calling Israel to separate themselves from certain things, this separation from something is connected to a calling that is best described as a separation for the sake of God's mission. Throughout the Scriptures, "faithfulness, love, justice, honesty, kindness and purity emerge as aspects of divine holiness that are to be replicated in the people of God".[11]

Holiness was also understood in terms of degrees or grades. Something or someone could be "most holy" or have some degree of lesser holiness based on proximity to God, either locationally or relationally. Holiness was tied to the cultic rituals of Israel's sacrificial system and bound by their laws (see especially the "Holiness Code" of Leviticus 17–26). Therein, God provided a means for people to be made "pure" or "clean", which was the opposite of "impure" or "unclean", and to move from "profane" to holy. The word "profane" should not be understood negatively. From a biblical perspective, it is simply a lack of holiness and can be translated as "common". Additionally, purity is primarily defined in terms of ritual cleanliness and not in terms of morality or ethics. To be profane and at the same time pure was the neutral state of most persons, places, or things.[12] Some action, positive or negative, had to transpire to move someone to either holy or impure. For example, a profane/pure person could become profane/impure by coming in contact with something that was unclean or by breaking a commandment. Their purity could be restored by making a suitable offering or partaking in ritual cleansing. Similarly, a profane/pure person could become a holy/pure person by participating in a ritual ceremony, dedication to God, or both.

It is easy to view this type of system as very mechanistic. That is to say, a system that operates without concern for the dispositions and motivations of the one who participates. This is the opposite of relational. This view was often the case for Israel since it was a simple way to avoid impurity. This led to the conclusion that the best way to prevent impurity was the legalistic observance of the law and complete separation from all the other nations (the extremes of this are seen in Ezra 9–10 and Nehemiah 13). Yet, throughout the Old Testament, we see significant signs of God's love for creation and desire for humanity to reciprocate and extend this love. The mere fact that God created humanity is proof of God's love. If we agree that God is whole (that is, not lacking anything at all) in God's self (within the pre-existent trinitarian relationship), then we can conclude that God did not need humanity (or any of creation). In other words, God does not need our worship or service. Therefore, the only reason for God to create is for the sake of love. Creation is an expansion of God's love. Additionally, we see God's continued love for humanity in the multiple covenants God established with Israel, who is called to be a blessing to the nations (Genesis 12:3).

COVENANT

In the ancient Near Eastern world, where the people of Israel were formed, a covenant was a formal and binding contract between two parties that included some type of religious ceremony, usually involving a sacrifice, to seal the agreement. There were two general types of covenants: 1) obligatory covenants, which were conditional, and 2) promissory covenants, which were unconditional. Some of the most important biblical covenants include the Noahic Covenant (Genesis 9:1-17); the Abrahamic Covenant (Genesis 12–17); the Mosaic Covenant (Exodus

19–24); The David Covenant (2 Samuel 7:4-17); and the New Covenant (Jeremiah 31:31-34; Hebrews 8:6-13).

It is important to understand several points related to these biblical covenants. First, the covenants are initiated by God as a means to establish lasting relationships with people. Second, most of these covenants are unconditional, meaning that regardless of specific human involvement, God would fulfil all God's promises "for the sake of (God's) holy name" (Ezekiel 36:22). Third, God's covenants are ultimately for the benefit of all humanity and part of fulfilling God's mission of redeeming and restoring all creation. Fourth, those who enter covenant with God are called to participate in God's mission of redeeming and restoring all creation. Fifth, people may choose to exclude themselves from God's covenants.

As part of the Mosaic Covenant, God gave the Ten Commandments as a guide to help Israel live in a genuine and sustainable relationship with Godself and others (Exodus 20). Even in the Levitical laws, we see God's desire for Israel to extend God's love to both Jews and Gentiles alike—"you shall love your neighbour as yourself" (Leviticus 19:18), and "you shall love the alien as yourself" (Leviticus 19:34). These are part of the outworking of God's invitation to "be holy, for I the Lord your God am holy" (Leviticus 19:2). God, holiness, and love are intrinsically and inseparably tied together.

Nevertheless, Israel's inability to keep the covenants in both their personal and social lives revealed the depths of individual and corporate sin. Ultimately, through the prophets, Israel came to understand its need for a Messianic Servant who would be "a light to the nations, that [God's] salvation may reach to the end of the earth" (Isaiah 49:6). This servant would take humanity's sins upon himself and suffer as God's righteous one in order to "make many righteous" (Isaiah 53:11). In other words, he would do what Israel could not, and in so doing, would provide a way for Israel to finally fulfil its covenant commitment and to live out holiness. This glorious messianic age, called the "Day of the Lord", would also usher in an age of the Holy Spirit where God would "pour out [God's] spirit on all flesh" enabling men and women, old and young, free and slave to prophesy, dream dreams, and see visions (Joel 2:28-29).

In God's abundant love and mercy, God would make "a new covenant." God would write the law upon their hearts so that "they shall all know [God], from the least of them to the greatest ... for [God] will forgive their iniquity, and remember their sin no more" (Jeremiah 31:31-34).

In the New Testament, it is clear that Jesus is this Messiah (which is another word for "Christ"), the anointed one of God. Through the Christ-event (incarnation, ministry, death, resurrection, and ascension), Jesus fully deals with the problem of heart corruption, making possible, through the indwelling Holy Spirit, a relationship of wholeness with God and neighbour. Purity of heart is offered as a realisable experience in this life. This is evident from the beginning, with the teaching of Jesus, and is then unfolded in the rest of the New Testament. As we look at the ministry of Jesus, we see that other people's impurities (real or supposed) did not make him unclean. This is a significant realisation. While the religious leaders assumed that any contact with someone or something that was unclean transmitted impurity, Jesus revealed that holiness was (and still is) more contagious.[13] In so doing, Jesus reclaimed the essence of holiness, realigning it to the character of God. The heart of holiness is well captured in Jesus's Great Commandment:

> "You shall love the Lord your God with all your heart, and with all your soul, and with all your mind." This is the greatest and first commandment. And a second is like it: "you shall love your neighbour as yourself." On these two commandments hang all the law and the prophets. (Matthew 22:37-40)

As we can see, rather than holiness being about separation, God's people are called to relationship—to connection, to presence, to incarnation!

Jesus also spoke about the gift of the Holy Spirit and the role that this Spirit would play in transforming God's people and making us holy. The Spirit resides within us and becomes our instructor. The Spirit allows us to become one with God, and to be one with each other, which in turn bears testimony to who Jesus is (see chapters 14–17 of John). One of the most significant passages on the work and power of the Holy Spirit is in Romans 8. Therein we learn that the Spirit: 1) sets us free from sin, death, and condemnation; 2) helps us to put to death our worldly desires, reshaping our desires towards the things of God; 3) gives us true resurrection life in the present; 4) makes us children of God and heirs with Christ, sharing in his glory; 5) and searches us, knows us, and prays on our behalf, even when we do not have the words to speak. In the work of the Spirit, we can clearly see God's love for us and God's desire for us to be wholly transformed by this love. This is holiness—moving "from one degree of glory to another" as we ever-increasingly reflect the image of Christ to others (2 Corinthians 3:18). Furthermore, becoming like Christ should lead us toward concrete actions. Those actions should resemble Christ's actions and the Kingdom ethic (see Matthew 5–7). As believers are reconciled to God, filled with the Holy Spirit, and transformed, they move into the places of pain, fear, and darkness to extend the holy love of God to the least of these (Matthew 25:31-46).

QUESTIONS FOR REFLECTION

1. Why is it important that we start with a biblical understanding of the doctrine of holiness?

2. How was holiness understood in the Old Testament?

3. In what ways does Jesus change the Old Testament understanding of holiness? In what ways does he affirm it?

CHAPTER 3

THE MEANING AND PURPOSE OF LIFE

The Bible says that the deep need to be in a positive relationship with God and others is at the very core of what it means to be human. This is clearly seen in the creation accounts of humanity, where male and female are deeply connected (Genesis 1:27) and where God announces that it is "not good" for Adam to be alone (Genesis 2:18). Sadly, much of Western culture (and in places where it has a substantial influence) emphasises the importance of independence, personal choice, and freedom. One's value is measured by what one achieves and owns, which brings a sense of acceptance and belonging. From childhood, people are often rewarded when they do well, and reproved when they do not, which places successful performance at the centre of personal identity. People are evaluated by how talented or how attractive they are, how much they earn or have, how educated, how successful, or how influential they are. Through these, and other markers, they establish their value and their sense of self-worth.

Almost universally, the present human condition is such that nothing is more natural than for people to seek happiness and fulfilment in those things that God has created, rather than in God. People often act as though other things and people exist to satisfy their needs and desires.

They are constantly on the lookout for the next person or product that is more desirable than the current one, seeking someone or something that holds out the promise of greater pleasure and satisfaction. People seek the approval of others before that of God, and when they do not believe they have such approval, it leads to deep feelings of failure, guilt, and shame. This, in turn, moves people to either try harder or simply give up, with both options resulting in a life less than what God would desire.

In many parts of the world, people no longer live in close contact with their family and birth community. It is common for people to leave rural settings and move to large cities. People can now live and make money without aid from their extended family. This growing economic independence inevitably leads to increased relational independence.

If humanity is to live as God intended, then people need each other! Being known just for achievements (or lack of them) is deeply unsatisfying, no matter how much people try to convince themselves otherwise. Every human being longs to be known and loved, to be seen and recognised as precious, affirmed and celebrated simply for being who they are. This desire to be loved requires the presence of others whose recognition and approval are important for each person's flourishing. Sadly, even this gets distorted, and people develop loyalty and affection for those who show the most loyalty and affection in return. Sometimes people try to buy love and acceptance by giving gifts or doing only what other people want. This is made worse by one's understanding of the nature of love. Love is often defined in terms of romantic feelings and sexual attraction, and the resulting actions are often very selfish—getting what one want from a relationship. This is not genuine love or genuine friendship, quite the opposite.

In humanity's actual condition, John Wesley believed that nothing "is more natural to us than to seek happiness in the creature instead of the Creator".[14]

THE SIN OF IDOLATRY

Idolatry is the worship of anything other than God, and it is at the core of Genesis 3, the narrative called the Fall. Adam and Eve desired to be like God (verses 3 and 4). In listening to the serpent, they elevated the authority of a created animal over that of the Creator. In a very real sense, this was an act of misdirected worship. Humankind has continued this downward spiral of sin, worshipping creation over Creator. In the words of the apostle Paul:

"[F]or though they knew God, they did not honor him as God or give thanks to him, but they became futile in their thinking, and their senseless minds were darkened. Claiming to be wise, they became fools; and they exchanged the glory of the immortal God for images resembling a mortal human being or birds or four-footed animals or reptiles" (Romans 1:21-23).

In the present technological age, we can add computers or smartphones to Paul's list as just another downward step into the worship of created things over the Creator. Through our obsession with technology, we have added physical isolation to our independence. We appear to prefer relationships that we can control, discard, and easily replace through "unfriending" or deleting people from our social media accounts. Sadly, Christians often fall into the same trap. Consequently, we see God as someone to control and manipulate into doing what we want, and who exists to meet our needs.

Hebrews 11:25 refers to the enjoyment of "the fleeting pleasures of sin". This reminds us that, like a young child with a toy, we are easily amused at first and satisfied by anything that catches our attention. These pleasures are called "fleeting" for a reason. Personal and community experience, as well as Scripture itself, remind us that these delights do not last very long. The parable of the prodigal son (Luke 15:11-32) is a perfect example of how quickly our fortunes can change and leave us desperate, deserted, and desolate. If we are "happy" with our current sources of pleasure and satisfaction, we will not be easily persuaded to give them up—even if they are harmful to our well-being. Convincing people that drugs are bad for their health rarely relieves relieves them of their addictions (legal or otherwise). Making rules and laws to change people's behaviour may be successful in the short term but rarely in the long term. Simply providing information and education is ineffective; authorities must try to find that which is more appealing and has a more desirable outcome, both personally and relationally. Advertisers rarely bother to disclose facts about why their product is better than the others. Instead, they try to create a desire associated with the perceived benefits of the experience or product that tempts us to change. If our present experience fails to deliver what it apparently promised, then we will seek someone or something else to provide the missing satisfaction.

God has created us in such a way that nothing outside of a loving relationship with God and neighbour can fully and finally satisfy and enable us to live without shame or guilt. What is it that will resonate with us and cause us to investigate whether life in God will be more satisfying than our present experience? What is it that will then keep us encouraged to develop the relationship to its full potential? The Psalmist invites us to "taste and see that the Lord is good" (Psalm 34:8). So, what would lure us to try the "taste test"? We are tempted to try some new taste when we are hungry, inquisitive, or intrigued by a possible new experience. Boredom and restlessness also make us open to new possibilities. It is at this point that we come to Wesley's oft-quoted statement from Augustine: God has made us for Godself, and our heart cannot rest until it rests in God.[15] This human desire for rest is a deep theological conviction for Wesley and it is the basis for his confidence in the appeal and power of the gospel.

SABBATH REST

The biblical concept of "sabbath" is introduced as a part of God's created order. Therein, God closely linked rest and holiness (Genesis 2:3). Sabbath is the fourth of only Ten Commandments given to the people to instruct them on how to properly love God and love others (Exodus 20:8-11). While there were times in Israel's history when this concept was observed legalistically, God's intention was more relational. Sabbath was a part of worship, a time to enjoy God's creation, which included receiving and caring for the other—the foreigner, the eunuch, and the outcast. Isaiah spoke of a glorious day when these "others" would "join themselves to the Lord, to minister to him, to love the name of the Lord, and to be his servants." And this was done simply by keeping the Sabbath, which was equated with holding fast to God's covenant (Isaiah 56:6). In other words, those who rested in God found true life. Jesus's invitation reiterates the call to Sabbath:

"Come to me all you that are weary and are carrying heavy burdens, and I will give you rest. Take my yoke upon you, and learn from me; for I am gentle and humble in heart, and you will find rest for your souls. For my yoke is easy, and my burden is light" (Matthew 11:28-30).

Ultimately, rest and happiness are identical in Wesley's understanding, since when our hearts are truly at rest in God, we are truly happy. Such rest keeps us centred on love and relationships as defined by God and not our culture, which brings the focus to a pure love for God from a pure heart and a single intention. The whole journey of salvation can be seen as a move from a selfish, self-centred love to loving God out of a pure heart, through the indwelling presence of the Holy Spirit.

John Wesley (along with many others) believed that God's essential nature is love. Over the course of his life and ministry, John Wesley demonstrated that this was biblical. He showed how this picture could be supported by the teaching of the Church and modelled in the lives of the faithful. Love is a relational quality, and God is a triune being (Father, Son, and Holy Spirit) who is in relationship with the other persons of the Godhead in an eternal communion. This love is generated by and flows from God's very being and is not something that arises from God finding another being or thing attractive. From the very beginning, the Christian story says every human being is the object of unconditional divine love (John 3:16) just because of his or her existence, not because of some special quality or ability that God finds attractive. The Bible constantly affirms that all people are special because God loves them, not that God only loves special people. God loves us without any regard to our status or merit, no matter how that is defined by our culture. As the Bible amply demonstrates, this divine love is a costly, self-giving love that reaches out to all, whoever and wherever they are, without distinction. Such a love is inherently transformative, and it cannot leave the one who is loved unchanged. To fully receive this love is to be in the image of God. To reject it is to see that image damaged and defaced.

GOD IS LOVE

First John 4:8 and 16 state that "God is love"; these verses equate God with love. In other words, God is not simply someone who has experienced or participated in this phenomenon we call love; rather, God is the source and fullness of all genuine love. This means that all the other attributes of God, including his sovereignty and holiness, are defined by God's love. God always acts out of love. The creation, the cross, and the coming restoration are all expressions of this love.

Since we have been created in the image of God, we too are relational beings and called to enter a relationship of holy love with God and with each other (Matthew 22:37-40). This is the essence of what it means to be a person. John Wesley wrote:

> For to this end was [humanity] created, to love God; and to this end alone, even to love the Lord [their] God with all [their] heart, and soul, and mind, and strength. But love is the very image of God: it is the brightness of his glory. By love [humanity] is not only made like God, but in some sense one with him. ... Love is perfect freedom ... Love is the health of the soul, the full exertion of all its powers, the perfection of all its faculties.[16]

In other words, to be human is firstly to experience the love of God and then to share it. This is where authentic meaning and purpose is found, and to live in love is the only way to truly flourish as our Creator intended. Such a love is defined by God's character and must be reflective of that character—being holy as God is holy (Leviticus 19:2). Such a love is free from all that is selfish and self-centred, while overflowing in the graces that are so clearly modelled in the life of Christ. In the original human creation, we received the fullness of God's love and had both the capacity and capability to fully return this love to God and our neighbour. As originally created, we were to be both holy and happy through knowing, loving, and enjoying God, the neighbours, and God's good creation. As Wesley wrote, to love God wholeheartedly "is the truest happiness, indeed the only true happiness which is to be found under the sun."[17] The Psalmist also declares: "How lovely is your dwelling place, O LORD of hosts! My soul longs, indeed it faints for the courts of the LORD; my heart and my flesh sing for joy to the living God. ... O LORD of hosts, happy is everyone who trusts in you" (Psalm 84:1-2, 12).

QUESTIONS FOR REFLECTION

1. In your culture, how are people valued? In what ways does the Christian gospel challenge that?

2. What does it mean to seek happiness in created things rather than in the Creator? Can you give some specific examples in your community?

3. Why is sin so attractive?

4. Wesley, like many others, affirms that God is love and that we are created in God's image. What difference does this make to your understanding of the value of every person?

CHAPTER 4

LOVE AND RELATIONSHIPS ARE PRIMARY

Jesus reminds us that the greatest commandment is to love God with our whole being and to love our neighbour as ourselves is closely related (Matthew 22:37-39). Additionally, the rest of the New Testament makes clear that we cannot truly love God if we do not love others (examples include Galatians 5:14, James 2:8, and 1 John 4:20-21). In other words, love and relationships are primary to who we are and to what we are called to do. Throughout Scripture, this relational God, who is love, has been reaching out to humanity and wooing it to Godself. The covenant with Abraham, the giving of the Ten Commandments, the Ark, priests, kings, and prophets are all examples of God's pursuit of humanity and evidence of God's desire to be in a rich relationship with them. Nowhere is this love more evident than in the incarnation, life, ministry, death, and resurrection of Jesus. The full Christ-event is a reminder that God is with us (Immanuel) and for us. Even so, such an amazing event can be reduced to a simple transaction and stripped of its profound relationality and love.

When the Gospel is reduced to "my salvation" and "me escaping hell", its true meaning and significance is lost. The oft-quoted words of John 3:16, must not be forgotten—"For God so loved the world that he gave his only Son, so that everyone who believes in him may not perish but may have eternal life." The Son was sent for no other reason than God's love for the whole cosmos (everyone and everything), and for no other purpose than enabling an everlasting relationship with God. This will ultimately lead to the whole creation being renewed and made fit for the people of God to live eternally with God (Revelation 21:5). As we become part of God's new creation people, we are at the same time called to a ministry of reconciliation (2 Corinthians 5:17-18). Christians are called to help restore broken relationships and to love all our neighbours in tangible ways (Luke 10:29-37). This point is especially made evident by Jesus in the Sermon on the Mount. Therein, we learn that we need other people to be able to do in reality that which has up to now only been theory.

THE SERMON ON THE MOUNT

Jesus's words in Matthew 5–7 provides us with a clear window into the Kingdom of Heaven (Kingdom of God). It is a sermon about true discipleship, and it centres on relational holiness. Over and over, Jesus tears down legalistic ways of observing the Torah (or law) to refocus his disciples on the heart of the Law, which is love. He redefines righteousness away from doing right based on the letter of the law and toward being right (and then doing out of this right being) based on compassion for the other (5:19-20). Christ-followers are motivated by love and should treat others, even their enemies, as they would like to be treated (7:12). Jesus's words are climaxed and encapsulated in Matthew 5:48—"Be perfect, therefore, as your heavenly Father is perfect." These words are an echo of Leviticus 19:2—"be holy, for I the Lord your God am holy"—and bring together the concepts of Christian perfection and holiness under the banner of love.

In the words of John Wesley:

> Christianity is essentially a social religion, and that to turn it into a solitary religion is indeed to destroy it. ... When I say this is essentially a social religion, I mean not only that it cannot subsist so well, but that it cannot subsist at all without society, without living and conversing with other [people].[18]

As we saw earlier, for many of us, the nature of love is defined by the media, with its notions of romantic love centred on feelings and fantasy, rather than the actual complex demands of lived relationships. We need to be reminded that it is God who reveals and defines love in all its fullness rather than our changing cultural ideals (regardless of which culture we come from). The true nature of love is displayed in the life, ministry, and sacrificial death of Jesus Christ. Christ's willingness to empty himself, take on human form, and become obedient to death (Philippians 2:5-7) provides us with the example to follow. We must start, continue, and end with God if we are to properly understand the nature of love. The Bible affirms that no one loves God or a neighbour without God first loving them (1 John 4:19). A person without God can only offer a damaged love to others, and this cannot be healed unless we first establish a right relationship with God.

Wesley said that the essential definition of being "a good Christian" was one who had experienced an inner change of heart and not simply one who achieved a set of external standards. Mere knowledge by itself cannot establish a genuine and lasting relationship with God; our heart's desires and affections must also be transformed. A genuine Christian experience involves both the head and the heart, and, biblically, it is the latter that is critical (Psalm 51:10). The heart is the source of all our inner motives and inclinations; it guides all our thoughts, words, and actions (Matthew 15:18-19). Our confidence to respond to God comes from having personally experienced the love of God, which in turn enables us to express the love of God to others. As Scripture reminds us, we love God because God first loved us (1 John 4:19). Without this personal experience of divine love, we would only know fear, shame, and guilt when we examine our relationship with God; there would be no basis for re-establishing a relationship with God on our part. Our trust in God (faith) arises as a response to the experience of God's love.

FAITH AND TRUST

The word "faith" is often equated with knowledge, and the action of being "faithful" is relegated to a mental exercise. However, from a biblical standpoint, faith is much more dynamic and relational. Both the

Hebrew (*emunah*) and Greek (*pistis*) words for faith denote trust, with the Hebrew word also carrying the notion of steadiness or reliability. Trust requires relationship. While this relationship may begin on a surface level as we learn about who this God is, deeper trust requires a deeper relationship. In other words, our faith is grounded in the reliability of God, and as we experience God's faithfulness, we can place our trust in God until this becomes a way of life—a life of faithfulness, and a life of holiness. As Scripture proclaims, "The one who is righteous will live by faith" (Romans 1:17; quoting from Habakkuk 2:4).

If love and trust are central, then Christianity is essentially about the heart and not the mind. It is about passion and not performance, about the purity of intention in a relationship and not the intellectual understanding of information as an academic exercise. This is fully outlined in 1 Corinthians 13 and many other passages in both the Old and New Testaments. Love both forms and empowers us to live authentic lives pleasing to God. It is both the fountain from which a Christlike character springs and the foundation of all our relationships. God desires a genuine connection with us in which we, through the Holy Spirit, return the love God first poured into our hearts. For Wesleyans, salvation involves a reciprocal relationship of love, for God will not force Godself upon us. Failure to return God's love causes us to experience what feels like a sense of God's gradual withdrawal, leading to an eventual fall into inward and then outward sin. While God's "goodness and faithful love will pursue [us] all the days of [our] lives" (Psalm 23:6, CEB), our lack of genuine engagement in relationship with God will inevitably lead to less reliance on the power of the Holy Spirit, which will draw us back into our own human frailties and inadequacies. In other words, without God's love in our hearts, we are powerless against sin.

LIFE IN THE VINE

Jesus provides us with an important illustration about life in God. He says, "I am the vine, you are the branches. Those who abide in me and I in them bear much fruit, because apart from me you can do nothing" (John 15:5). Jesus is the source of all true life and power. It is only as we abide in him, through the Holy Spirit, that we can be transformed, do good, and resist sin. As Peter wrote, "His divine power has given us everything needed for life and godliness" (2 Peter 1:3). In other words, holiness is impossible apart from God. Nevertheless, God does not force this relationship upon us. We have the ability to make a conscious choice to live a life detached from the vine and, thus, disconnected from the power of the Holy Spirit.

QUESTIONS FOR REFLECTION

1. What is significant about the Greatest Commandment telling us to love God and our neighbour?

2. How does the love of God differ from our culture's definition of love?

3. Faith is defined primarily as trust in this chapter. Why is that important when we think about relationships?

CHAPTER 5

LOVE MISDIRECTED (THE PROBLEM)

Wesley was convinced that authentic love required human freedom—a genuine ability to say yes or no to the relationship God offers. A love that was forced, either through the way we were created or by overwhelming pressure from a greater power, would not be love at all. Without freedom there is no real value to our ability to understand and evaluate a situation before choosing a course of action. If we are not free, then the whole idea of personal choice and personal responsibility is meaningless. We would simply be shaped by outside forces and could not be held personally accountable for anything. This is at the heart of the Wesleyan rejection of the Calvinist understanding of election and predestination.

ELECTION AND PREDESTINATION

Wesleyans do not reject election and predestination. They are terms and concepts, after all, in the Bible. What Wesleyans do reject are certain interpretations of the scriptural references that come together to form a particular theological understanding where God arbitrarily chooses ("elects") some to be predestined for heaven and some to be predestined for hell. A major difficulty with this viewpoint is that it dismisses the multitude of biblical passages that express God's love for all of creation

(John 3:16), "not wanting any to perish, but all to come to repentance" (2 Peter 3:9).

One of the clearest expressions of Israel's election in the Old Testament is Deuteronomy 7:6—"For you are a people holy to the Lord your God; the Lord your God has chosen you out of all the peoples on earth to be his people, his treasured possession." Nevertheless, Israel's election was not an end in itself. They were chosen for a task, namely, to bless "all the other families of the earth" (Genesis 12:3) by being a "light to the nations" so that God's salvation "may reach to the end of the earth" (Isaiah 49:6). Throughout Scripture, those chosen by God are not selected for their own sake, nor because they possess special skills or abilities; usually quite the opposite. They are chosen to join God in the mission of bringing salvation and restoration to all creation (see the companion book in the series: *Entering the Mission of God*[19]).

In the New Testament, references to election and predestination are integrally tied to God's purposes and do not expressly exclude anyone. Instead, they are directed toward those who have already responded to God's all-inclusive grace and have chosen to place their trust in this God. Notice the things God has chosen and predestined for his followers. We are chosen "to be holy and blameless before him in love" and predestined "for adoption as his children" (Ephesians 1:4-5). We are "predestined to be conformed to the image of his Son" and told that "those whom he predestined he also called ... justified ... and ... glorified" (Romans 8:29-30). The blessings bestowed on followers of Christ are not self-serving or individualistic. Our experience of God's love, holiness, and transformation to Christlikeness is for the sake of extending these realities to others. "So election is not the means of leaving out other people but the means of drawing them in."[19]

At the core of the God-human relationship (and every other relationship) must be a genuinely free choice; otherwise humans are simply biological machines or helpless victims of some irresistible greater power. This is not to deny the impact our biology and environment have on how we make decisions, but they are not the ultimate reasons for our choices. Wesleyans believe that God's wisdom, power, and goodness are best seen in governing us as humans made in God's image, with the gifts of understanding, will, and freedom, and that God will not overrule these. If we are not free to accept or reject God's loving offer of a new life in Christ, then we cannot be held accountable for our thoughts, words, or actions. The Bible's teaching on personal and community judgement would be pointless since we could neither be rewarded for right choices nor penalized for wrong ones. In fact, we could not be judged as morally good or morally evil, since we were simply fated by biology and life circumstances to think, speak, and act as we did.

In the light of this, Wesleyans believe that God could not compel humanity to be saved without destroying or denying its ability to choose. If God did this, then God would be destroying the very nature of the creation God had made. Wesley agreed with Calvin that the immediate consequence of Adam and Eve's sin was the loss of human freedom and an inability to choose to return to God because humanity was now in total bondage to sin. However, Wesley disagreed with Calvin about God's response to that situation. Calvin's answer was that God personally and irresistibly chose the people who would be saved and gave them the grace of salvation, which they could not reject or lose. But Wesley felt this was to deny an essential quality that makes us human—the power to choose. Wesley argued that God gave a type of grace that he called "preventing" or "prevenient" grace through Christ to every person from the beginning of their life and this counteracted the bondage to sin, enabling a genuine choice to be made. This grace does not force a choice but enables it. If I help a person with crippled legs to stand, that does not mean that I am the one to decide what direction he or she must go. The choice is his or hers. In the same way, a person may choose to resist the offer of God's love and relationship, or he or she may accept it. People are responsible for their choices, and the ability to choose ensures that their love and relationships are the authentic outcomes of their personal knowledge, motives, and choices.

THEOLOGICAL FRAMEWORK: CALVINIST VERSUS WESLEYAN

The Calvinist theological framework can be understood using the acronym T.U.L.I.P.

- Total Depravity – As a result of original sin, humanity is fundamentally corrupt, incapable of being righteous and of choosing God.

- Unconditional Election – God's choice of who will be saved is not based on human action or condition. In God's sovereignty, God chooses whomever God pleases.
- Limited Atonement – Christ's atonement is limited to those whom God has predestined for salvation.
- Irresistible Grace – Those whom God has elected are incapable of resisting God's grace; they have no choice in the matter.
- Perseverance of the Saints – Since God's grace is irresistible, the elect cannot fall from grace; God will always preserve them.

To highlight the difference between the Calvinist and Wesleyan (and Arminian) positions, the same five points are addressed and clarified from a Wesleyan perspective.

- Total Depravity with Prevenient Grace – Humanity is fundamentally corrupt because of sin and thus unable to be righteous or choose God on their own. But God's prevenient grace gives humanity the ability to choose or reject God.
- Conditional Election – God's love for all prevents God from forcing salvation on anyone. As a result, God's election is based on those who willingly choose God; thus, election is conditioned on faith in God.
- Unlimited Atonement – God desires that all people will be saved and transformed. Christ's atonement is for all, but the full benefits of this atonement are only experienced by those who believe.
- Free (but Resistible) Grace – As a result of Prevenient Grace, each person may freely accept or resist God's wooing.
- Assurance of the Saints – Since grace is resistible, followers may make conscious choices to walk away from God's saving grace, but believers can be assured that God will not remove God's grace.

Wesley doubted that Adam would have chosen evil, knowing it to be such. However, he might have mistaken evil for good since he did not know everything. The Bible affirms that humans were not created knowing everything (because that would make us divine), so ignorance cannot, in itself, be evil. Wesley was clear that ignorance only becomes sinful when one wilfully refuses to accept or learn from the truth that God gives. While ignorance may lead to wrong choices and harmful outcomes, these choices are only sinful if the person could have known and acted otherwise.

Imagine this scenario. I approach a bridge across a deep ravine and have no reason to doubt its safety. I can set out to cross it with a good conscience. However, unknown to me, the anchor point at the other end has failed. When I get partway over, the bridge collapses, and I am severely injured by my fall into the ravine. In this case, I acted in good faith based on the information I had, but that did not prevent me suffering an injury. If, on the other hand, as I approach the bridge, I see a prominent notice warning me that the bridge is unsafe and likely to fail, and decide to ignore it and try to cross, then I have wilfully and deliberately ignored the information. I am at fault for my own injuries.

Similarly, we can see that the choice made in the garden by Adam and Eve was not due to their limited knowledge, because God had clearly warned them not to eat from that tree. However, doubting God's love and an unwillingness to continue to trust God was at the centre of their choice to sin. The serpent explicitly sought to undermine their trust by casting doubt on God's words and intentions—that God was deliberately denying them something good and desirable (Genesis 3:5). This lies at the core of a Wesleyan understanding of the nature of sin. Sin is something that people wilfully and deliberately choose to do or not do, based on their informed understanding. Because of intention, the essential nature of sin is seen as a deliberate and willful choice to harm the relationship with God (or neighbour); its "voluntariness" is a crucial part of Wesley's definition of terms. To return to the analogy of the bridge, choosing to try and cross in the first instance was not "a sin" (I had no way of knowing the bridge was faulty). In the second case, it was "a sin" because I had a clear knowledge of the consequences of my choice and deliberately chose to ignore the warning. In both situations, the actual outcome was the same (I was injured), although the intended outcome was not.

Prior to the Fall, when divine love filled people's hearts, these people would have "naturally" thought, said, and done that which was in harmony with God's character. Ever since the Fall, human beings have exercised their freedom to satisfy themselves rather than live in harmony and integrity with God. Beginning in the early chapters of Genesis, God revealed what was required for humans to flourish and the consequences of not receiving God's offer of salvation. In time, God gave the Law which made humanity aware of how far short of their original creation they now come.

THE LAW

The Ten Commandments (Exodus 20:1-17; Deuteronomy 5:6-21) were given to the people of Israel after they came out of slavery in Egypt. At the time, the people had very little understanding of who this God was and what God desired from them. This law (and those that followed) provided them with guidelines for living in a relationship with God and with each other. The Law helped them understand the kind of God they were worshiping, and, over time, revealed their own inadequacies and inability to live out holy love apart from God. The law was never intended as a means of salvation. It was not the answer to our problem, but the means of demonstrating the problem (Romans 7:7-10) and pointing us towards the only solution—Christ (Romans 7:25a). In Christ, the law is not negated (Matthew 5:17). It is brought to its proper interpretation and summarised in the Great Commandment of loving God and our neighbour with our whole being (Matthew 22:37-40). As Christians, we are not imprisoned by the law; we are justified by faith in Christ's faith-fullness (Galatians 3:21-29). Still, as we abide in Christ and through the power of the Holy Spirit, we are motivated by love and strive toward good works to fulfill "the perfect law, the law of liberty" (James 1:22-25).

Christ, and not the law, is the only true solution; and the salvation that happens in Christ enables the restoration of choice that had been lost in the garden. Wesleyans believe that God graciously enables us to choose or reject a relationship with God without robbing us of the freedom essential to a moral agent. Wesley called this assistance preventing (prevenient) grace, because it restored to humanity the ability to choose or reject God. Prevenient grace is the critical point of difference between the Wesleyan and Calvinist theological frameworks, and it impacts their understanding of the possibilities of grace in this life. Furthermore, it lies at the heart of their disagreement over entire sanctification.

QUESTIONS FOR REFLECTION

1. Why is freedom so important for love to be genuine?

2. What are the key differences between a Calvinist and a Wesleyan understanding of the account of the Fall in Genesis 3?

3. Why will trying to become holy by keeping the law prove to be unsuccessful?

CHAPTER 6

LOVE RENEWED

As we saw in Exploring a Wesleyan Theology, our relationship with God after the Fall is now defined by our own selfish desires, attitudes, and values. We would much rather find pleasure and satisfaction in created things than in a life with our Creator. We are happy to be religious, spiritual, and look, speak, and act like good Christians in serving others if we can have the final say. We are much more interested in self-satisfaction and self-glorification than desiring to please God above all else. Wesley identified this inclination—self-centredness and self-will—as "in-being sin". Though God always offers us sufficient grace to overcome it, we prefer to indulge our own wants, priorities, and values rather than cooperating with that grace to be delivered from the power of in-being sin. We are happy to be Christians as long as we get to set the limits of what God can ask us to do. It is this "double-mindedness" (James 1:8; 4:8) that impacts our new life in Christ and robs us of experiencing the full benefits of Christ's atoning death. Loving ourselves above all other loves makes it impossible to believe that life in all its fullness is genuinely found in loving God with all our heart, soul, mind, and strength. In the daily struggles of life, we wonder if it is even possible to be delivered from such a depth of selfishness and self-centredness? Wesley and his successors firmly believe that we can experience a full deliverance from the power of in-being sin in this life. Wesleyans believe that God will deal with in-being sin (sometimes called "the root") just as thoroughly as God deals with the sinful acts ("the fruit") that flow from it through a subsequent "work of grace" that God has promised in Scripture. We are confident that what God has promised in Scripture, God will surely fulfill (Ezekiel 12:28; Philippians 1:6). God does not mock us by holding out an offer of deliverance that God never intends to give.

Entire sanctification should be seen and understood from several perspectives. We can talk about it in terms of purity of intention, in which we dedicate our whole life to God, desiring with all our being to please God in every way. We can also talk about having the "mind of Christ" (1 Corinthians 2:16) that enables us to walk as he walked. This ties into the biblical notion of the "circumcision of the heart" that purifies us from all inward and outward pollution and renews us in Christlikeness. It can also be seen as loving God with our whole heart and our neighbour as ourselves. All of these are biblical concepts that refer to that same experience of grace. This experience of entire sanctification is not our final salvation (often called "glorification"), as that awaits our resurrection and the re-creation of all things by God. Nor is entire sanctification a state of holiness devoid of involuntary transgressions because it depends on a current, intimate relationship with Christ, in which the quality of love is continually able to be enriched, resulting in a deeper transformation and life of service.

A right relationship with God begins with the new birth (regeneration), which is a complete work in itself. In that moment, we are forgiven, reconciled, and born again into the family of God. We are no longer children of darkness and death, but children of light and life through Jesus Christ.

REGENERATION

The theological understanding of regeneration is developed from multiple passages in the New Testament and has individual, corporate, and cosmic ramifications. The most well known of these is the dialogue between Jesus and Nicodemus (John 3:1-21), which centres around the need for people to be "born from above" or "born of the Spirit" (also known as being "born again"). Jesus is speaking about a spiritual birth whereby persons enter the Kingdom of God (in the present) as they place their trust in him. Likewise, Paul affirms that God saves us "by the washing of regeneration and renewing by the Holy Spirit" (Titus 3:5, NASB), and Peter proclaims that God "has given us a new birth into a living hope" through Christ (1 Peter 1:3). In Matthew 19:28, Jesus speaks of the "regeneration" of all things at the end of the age, which is echoed in Paul's references to "new creation" (2 Corinthians 5:17; Galatians 6:15), and in 2 Peter 3:13 and Revelation 21:1, where each speaks of "a new heaven and a new earth". From the biblical evidence, we can conclude the following three truths about regeneration: "First and foremost, it is an act of the triune God—Father, Son, and Spirit. Second, it is based in a sustained relationship with this triune God. Third, its end goal is wholeness and holiness in the individual, the corporate church, and all the created order."[21]

This moment of regeneration is the beginning of our sanctification in which we believers are being transformed into the image of Christ and made genuinely holy. There is a process of sanctification that both precedes and follows entire sanctification, which is the "moment" when remaining sin (in-being sin) is expelled by God's love filling our hearts through the work of the Holy Spirit. Since Paul and the other New Testament writers applied the term "sanctified" to all Christians and not merely to those who had victory over all sin, Wesley was careful to qualify sanctification with such terms as "wholly" or "entirely" when referring to this fuller work. The danger is to confuse entire sanctification with regeneration, which would make the starting point the full extent of the journey.

At the moment of our new birth, the power of in-being sin (the sinful inclination) is decisively broken, but it is not yet completely defeated. Sins are often described as chains, wounds, diseases, and debts, all of which need a subsequent work of grace to fix, but they no longer need to control our lives. By God's grace, we Christians are enabled to live in the power of Christ and to know a real deliverance from the power of sin—no longer do we need to sin in thought, word, and deed every day. A faithful relationship with God, grounded in grace, is possible from the very beginning. This is because its essential nature has to do with love and trust, not duty and performance. Wesley believed that those in

Christ did not continue in willful (intentional) sin as they continued to walk in the power of the Spirit. Furthermore, they were not under condemnation for the residue of sin (Romans 8:1) as long as they did not yield to sin in the present. To continue in willful sin is to demonstrate you are not living as a child of God, for even "babes in Christ" are so far perfect as not to sin (or at least, commit outward sin) due to the presence of the Holy Spirit.[22]

As we allow the Spirit to work in our lives, the depth and extent of this transformation will increase. This moment-by-moment walk of obedience to Christ is a process that extends over our whole life. Very often, in the early days of our new life in Christ, we feel as though the power of sin has not only been broken, but that it has, in fact, been taken away completely. However, there comes a time when we become too aware that we still prefer to live life on our own terms rather than on God's. It does not take long before the new Christian knows that while the power of sin may be broken, it is still very much active, and any temptation finds a ready supporter here. This leads to both inward sin in thought, motive, and desire, as well as outward failure when the person commits actual sins in word and deed. This sets up an inner struggle between the prompting of the Spirit to live as God desires and the prompting to satisfy our own desires. Sometimes we listen to the Spirit, and sometimes we listen to our own selfish nature; sometimes we live in victory, and sometimes we live in defeat (Matthew 26:41). The Spirit does give us gradual victory over this inward inclination and does enable us to know a greater and greater level of deliverance; that is, if we keep our faith in Christ, walk in his ways, and do not yield to destructive doubts and fears.

DOUBTS

In the New Testament, several different Greek words are translated as "doubt" in English. One set of words (usually *diakrinō*) pertains to the mind—thinking through something, then judging it as uncertain or untrue. The other set of words (*apisteō* and its cognates) connects more to the heart and are better translated as unbelief or unbelieving. These usually refer to a lack of trust in God, or more specifically in Jesus. As we survey the several references by Jesus to both kinds of doubt, we quickly see that "doubting" is not evil. It is not even necessarily a bad thing; it is simply part of our current reality. Some people doubt because they lack the information and understanding needed to move beyond these doubts. Others doubt because they either have not encountered Jesus, or have yet to experience a true relationship with him. While Jesus often appears frustrated by the disciples's doubting (e.g., Mark 9:19; Matthew 14:31), he nevertheless encourages all people toward a more profound knowledge and deeper faith in God (e.g., Mark 11:23; John 20:27).

Since Christianity is about a dynamic relationship with the triune God, we should always strive toward more understanding and deeper trust in Christ. This is how we grow in love and holiness. Doubts become destructive when we linger in them too long without seeking greater understanding or deeper trust in God. Any doubts that stop us from genuinely engaging with God are destructive. God invites us to bring all our doubts, fears, frustrations, and troubles to God. God is not afraid of our doubts; God is big enough to bear the burden of these doubts and to move us toward a deeper faith.

For many of us Christians, this is our daily experience—moments of rejoicing in Christ and moments of guilt and shame when we give in once more to our own self-centred desires. Many Protestant churches believe that we will have total victory over this in-being sin before we see Christ face to face but that this deliverance from the power of sin will only occur just before our death. We will then be holy through and through in every aspect of our life and relationships. This is a wonderful assurance. However, is that all we can hope for? A life-long cycle of victory and defeat before final deliverance at death?

Wesley did not dispute that this was undoubtedly the experience of many (if not most) Christians, but that did not mean it was all that could be expected. He would encourage us to keep our focus on Christ and the depths of his pardoning love. Beyond that, he would also encourage us to believe the promises of God that there is a real and present deliverance from this remaining sinful inclination. We are to continue to be faithful in prayer, in worship, in service, while all the time claiming God's promise of filling our hearts with God's love and thereby expelling all sin.

The Wesleyan position is that we need not wait till the end of life for us to experience the fullness of God's love in our hearts. Based on the promises of God found throughout Scripture (and in the New Testament particularly), Wesley argued for a subsequent work of grace after our new birth. This act of God would see love expelling sin and enabling the obedient Christian to know a heart cleansed from all self-centredness and self-will. Wesley was confident that God promised deliverance from in-being sin in this life, not just at death. The foundation for all Wesley's claims was the Scripture itself and that there were clear promises of such a full deliverance in a range of passages.[23] Wesley believed entire sanctification could be experienced before death because the commands of Scripture were addressed to the living and not the dead.[24]

Wesley saw actual examples of the wholly sanctified in the Apostle John and all those he referred to in 1 John 4:17. Wesley concluded, "if the love of God fill all the heart, there can be no sin there."[25] This quality of relationship marks the beginning of an ever-deepening life in Christ, and it is this stage of our journey that Wesley called "Christian perfection", which is always described in terms of love. He wrote:

> Christian perfection is that love of God and neighbour, which implies deliverance from all sin ... [it] is received merely by faith ... it is given instantaneously, in one moment. ... [and] we are to expect it, not at death, but every moment; that now is the accepted time, now is the day of this salvation.[26]

Wesley believed that John confirmed that Christians can experience "perfect love" in this life, not just at the moment of death (1 John 1:5-6, 9; 3:7-10; 4:17).[27] In his view, this is where the promises given in passages like Deuteronomy 30:6, Psalm 51:10, and Ezekiel 36:25-28 are fulfilled.[28] This belief is confirmed in the New Testament, where some believers are clearly addressed as "perfect" (e.g., 1 Corinthians 2:6, 15; 13:10; Philippians 3:15; Galatians 6:1).

PERFECT/PERFECTION

The words *telos* and *teleios* are part of a Greek word group that has a large range of meanings. For example, they refer to end, completion, cessation, maturity, wholeness, fulfilment, and goal. The modern understanding (based on the Latin word) of the words "perfect" and "perfection" means "without defect or blemish" (1 Peter 1:19). This meaning can be found in this word group (and in Scripture), but this modern understanding of *telos* and *teleios* is not the only way to understand the concept. Christ was the only human to have fulfilled this definition of the word (Hebrews 2:10; 5:9).[29] Even as we consider the various animal sacrifices found in the Old Testament (Exodus 12:5; Leviticus 22:21), we can readily recognise that these animals were not perfect in the modern sense of the word. Instead, we could say they were "fit for purpose"; that is, they were well suited for the role they needed to fulfil. When the New Testament speaks of perfection in relation to believers, it is strongly connected to God's love. We are told that God is love and that as we "love one another, God lives in us, and his love is perfected in us" (1 John 4:12). Jesus even connects perfection with our love for our enemies (Matthew 5:43-48). God's love working in us and through us moves us toward maturity, putting an end to childish ways (1 Corinthians 13:11) and growing in "the unity of the faith and the knowledge of the Son of God, to maturity, to the measure of the full stature of Christ" (Ephesians 4:13). Time and time again, we as the Church are called to a kind of perfection and maturity that align our thinking and doing with those of the Kingdom. We are given purpose in our perfection, and this purpose is to partner with God in completing Christ's work on earth (John 4:34; 1 John 2:5-6; Colossians 3:14-17).

In Wesleyan understanding, this work of grace is a genuine deliverance from in-being sin with its corrupting influence that impacts every area of our lives. It is important to remember that in-being sin is not a "thing" to be removed, but an inclination, a heart's desire, a disease that needs to be remedied, restoring us to full moral and spiritual health. This can be pictured in medical terms in which the sanctifying work of the Spirit (Ephesians 5:25-27; Hebrews 13:12; 1 John 1:7) "heals" us from the infection (sin pictured as a disease, yeast, or virus, that infects the whole person, a leprosy that corrupts every power and faculty). Entire sanctification is then pictured as spiritual health fully restored. Just as our physical health must be maintained "moment-by-moment" through the continual use of such things as a proper diet, exercise, and hygiene, so our "spiritual health" must be continually maintained through obedience to the clear commands of Scripture and practising a range of spiritual disciplines. To disregard these elements is to become diseased again. and to avoid this requires vigorous vigilance.

Another biblical model is entire sanctification as the work of the victorious Christ. This stresses the presence of the triumphant and glorified Christ, who now reigns in our hearts as Prophet, Priest, and King, enabling us to be holy through the dynamic presence of the Holy Spirit (e.g., Romans 6:1-11; 8:1-17; Galatians 5:16-25). Remember that Christ does not give us life separate from himself, but in and with himself (John 15). Like the healing metaphor, it stresses that we always need Christ in this way; no matter how "holy" we are, it is always the result of a moment-by-moment union with Christ through the Spirit.

The greatest challenge to Wesley's understanding of Christian perfection came from those in the Calvinist theological tradition. The Calvinists denied that it was possible for any human being to perfectly conform to God's law in every particular. According to them, any lack of conformity to God's perfect law by our actions or failure to act—in word, thought, or deed—is sin. This means that all live in sin until released by death. This was a point that troubled many within Methodism in Wesley's day, and it continues to be a point of contention today. Wesley readily confessed that all humans breach the "Adamic law", the absolute law of God, and that any falling short of this law is sin in this sense and, therefore, needs forgiveness. There is no sinless perfection while we are in this body on this side of resurrection.

Wesley recognised that real issue is how we define sin. Under one set of definitions (sin is a voluntary breach of the law of love), perfection was a defensible concept; under another set (any coming short of God's law is sin), it was not. This required Wesley to distinguish between "sin properly so called" and "involuntary transgressions". The former was voluntary; it was wilfully chosen. Therefore, we are liable for the wrong ,and we deserve condemnation. The latter were not wilfully chosen, and, consequently, we are not liable; they do not bring condemnation. Wesley agreed with his critics that Adam, as originally created (before the Fall), was perfectly capable of meeting all of God's requirements since he had no defect in his body, understanding, or affections. He was able to understand clearly, judge truly, reason correctly, and act perfectly in total conformity to God's demands. Thus, God could (and did) demand that Adam perfectly keep all that God required of him.

However, after the first sin and its consequences (Genesis 3), humans are no longer in this state and cannot possibly perfectly live up to all that God requires. That would mean that a loving God would require of us something that we could no longer do, and sinning in thought, word, and deed every day of our earthly existence would be unavoidable. Wesley rejected such a picture of God and God's requirements, believing instead that the gospel offered us a different framework for our relationship with God in our current state—a relationship grounded in grace rather than in law.

In his sermon, "The Righteousness of Faith", Wesley clarified his understanding of the distinction between the "covenant of works" as applied in the original creation setting and the "covenant of grace" that is applicable now. Under the former nothing but absolute perfection and obedience would do in order to be accepted by God, which is impossible for all humans as they are now constituted.[30] Wesley firmly believed that righteousness in Scripture is not defined in legal terms as obedience to law or conformity to an absolute standard, but as God's love expressed in a right relationship with Godself and subsequently with all other persons. People were created with the fullness of God's love and the ability to fully return that love to God and other creatures.[31]

RIGHTEOUSNESS
The biblical understanding of righteousness is often interpreted through a Greco-Roman lens, which is where we get the legal aspect of the

term. In ancient Greek understanding, righteousness (Greek root *dikē*) was tied to the virtue of being "just" or "right", especially with regard to the law. Nevertheless, both the Old Testament and New Testament uses of righteousness are tied to its Jewish background. In the Old Testament, God's righteousness (Hebrew root *sdq*) is governed by God's "steadfast love" or "covenant faithfulness" (*hesed*—Psalm 33:5). God is faithful to Israel because God has entered into a covenant relationship with them. God's righteousness is, therefore, measured by God's faithfulness to this relationship, regardless of whether Israel remains faithful (see the story of Hosea and 2 Timothy 2:13).

In other words, righteousness is first and foremost a relational concept. This is illustrated in the story of Abram (Abraham) in Genesis 15. Abram's righteousness came as a result of his trust (faith) in God (cf. Galatians 3:6-9). Yet, as Genesis 15 clearly illustrates, Abram's faith was far from perfect. What was perfect was God's faithfulness to Abram in reassuring him of the promises God had already made. Abram took this bit of faith and moved forward in obedience. From a human perspective, righteousness requires faith and obedience, but these are integrally tied to a relationship with God. God's righteousness, if we allow it, will transform us and make us holy. As the apostle John writes, "if we walk in the light as he himself is in the light, we have fellowship with one another, and the blood of Jesus his son cleanses us from all sin" (1 John 1:7).

Perfect Love and Imperfect Bodies

The Wesleyan position rejects any notion of "sinless perfection", and in Wesley's Preface to his *Hymns and Sacred Poems,* he listed some twenty-six scripture passages to refute this charge.[32] He affirmed that he upheld the doctrines of the Church of England: "the perfection I hold is so far from being contrary to the doctrine of our Church that it is exactly the same which every clergyman prays every Sunday: 'Cleanse the thoughts of our hearts by the inspiration of thy Holy Spirit, that we may perfectly love thee, and worthily magnify thy holy name.' I mean neither more nor less than this".[33] By perfection "I mean 'perfect love', or the loving God with all our heart, so as to rejoice evermore, to pray without ceasing, and in everything to give thanks. I am convinced every believer may attain this".[34] Wesley was careful to clarify that he did not preach either angelic or Adamic perfection.

The highest perfection which [we] can attain while the soul dwells in the body does not exclude ignorance and error, and a thousand other infirmities. Now from wrong judgments wrong words and actions will often necessarily flow. ... Nor can I be freed from a liableness to such a mistake while I remain in a corruptible body. A thousand infirmities in consequence of this will attend my spirit till it returns to God who gave it. And in numberless instances it comes short of doing the will of God as Adam did in paradise.[35]

The heart of the difference between Calvinism and Wesleyanism is found in this link between love and relationship. Firstly, it affects our understanding of the possibilities of grace in this life. Secondly, it informs our understanding of whether perfection might be experienced before death. Though God's work of salvation in this present life is able to deliver us from the reign of sin in our hearts, it does not bring about a full deliverance from all the consequences of personal sins as well as our sins as a group, let alone the devastation wrought on the rest of God's created order. There is an "already—not yet" tension in Wesley's understanding of Christ's work.

We already experience a great deliverance from the power of sin, but it is not yet a final deliverance in which all things will be made new. He clearly limits perfection in this life to love—the love of God received in its fullness and shared by grace with the neighbour. He repeatedly writes that there is no perfection in knowledge or freedom from ignorance in this life, nor from the mistakes that arise from them. We never have knowledge that is perfect in extent (though we can be sure of things essential to salvation). This limitation leads to misjudgments of people and actions and our understanding and application of Scripture. None of us are infallible, thus, this side of resurrection, we are always open to error, ignorance, and physical, mental, and emotional infirmities. All of these can be present in a relationship without the relationship being broken. What breaks a loving relationship is intentionally thinking, speaking, or acting (or intentionally failing to think, speak, or act) in ways that are designed to harm the one we love and damage the relationship. There is a vast difference in a loving relationship between intentionally hurting another and accidently hurting the one we love.

As human parents, we understand the difference between the willful defiance of our child that is intended to cause pain, and the accidental behaviour that was never meant to do so. There is a vast difference between our young child throwing their meal on the ground because they do not want to eat it and the child accidentally dropping the meal on the ground. Even though the result is the same in both cases, a good parent reacts differently to willful defiance and accidental damage. In both cases, the appropriate response from the child is to express sorrow and offer to clean it up, but only in the first case will the child experience genuine guilt and shame because it was intentional. If we as human parents can see that difference and respond accordingly, how much more can God?

Likewise, in this life, we are not free from bodily infirmities. The physical nature of the body living in a disordered and corrupted environment makes it liable to weakness, sickness, disorder, pain, and death. Even mature Christians deal with the consequences of weak and limited understanding: confusion, inaccuracy, mistakes, false judgments, and wanderings of imagination. These inward or outward imperfections are not of a moral nature and so are not sin because there is no condemnation for things where we have no power to choose otherwise. Wesley sought to demonstrate from Scripture that there was no condemnation for "sins of infirmity" due to the realities of our human condition since the Fall. He agreed that both sins and infirmities were deviations from the perfect will of God and so needed Christ's gracious atonement. Even so, he insisted that the latter brought no condemnation.[36] This was because he felt the Scriptures gave no grounds for believing that God condemned us for thoughts, words, and actions beyond our power to prevent them. Based on his study of Scripture, he reasoned that condemnation was experienced only to the degree that the will was involved.[37]

Given the damage that sin has done to the human race, we can no longer keep the original covenant of works, which required absolute obedience and perfect performance. However, that does not mean that we cannot keep the covenant of grace. Unlike those from the Calvinist tradition, we believe that the God of love has now offered us a covenant of grace that suits the realities of the present human condition. We can, by God's grace alone, keep this covenant that is centred in love and relationship. This means that the requirement for perfection this side of death can only ever be a relative perfection. This is confirmed in Wesley's understanding of Paul's teaching in 1 Thessalonians 5:23: "As if he [Paul] had said, '[You] shall enjoy as high a degree of holiness as is consistent with your present state of pilgrimage ... loving him with all your heart (which is the sum of all perfection)' ".[38] For God to hold us to a standard of performance we can no longer achieve would be a violation of love. Both covenants are suited to the capacities and abilities of their subjects, with a corresponding responsibility and accountability.

All of this means that life in the present body is still subject to errors and mistakes that arise solely from our physical and mental condition. These defects impact our quality of life and relationships. Nevertheless, we are not doomed to a life of endless sinning and defeat. Wesley strongly rejected such a pessimistic conclusion. He argued that all the requirements of the law were met fully in Christ, who had now established the law of faith, so that the one who believed in him would be fully accepted by God.[39] The law of faith established by Christ was fulfilled by love: "Faith working or animated by love is all that God now requires of [people]. He has substituted (not sincerity, but) love, in the room of angelic perfection".[40] It is likely that we will still offend against this law, since mistakes and harmful words, actions, and thoughts may spring from a heart of love.

Wesley reminded his people that they did not have a "stock of holiness" that was their own. Instead, they must depend in every moment upon Christ; they always needed Christ's atonement, intercession, and advocacy with the Father. Wesley was careful to maintain that we Christians never achieved a state of grace in which we no longer needed the priestly work of Christ. Christians no longer needed the atonement to reconcile them to God or to restore God's favour but rather to continue it. Wesley agreed that to give up a continuing atonement was in effect to give up "perfection", but we need not do either.[41] Living in a corrupted body did mean that "mistakes" would arise, not from a defect of love, but a defect of knowledge. As long as there was "no concurrence of the will," there was no sin.[42] He was positive that a relationship with God centred in love could be unbroken if the Christian acknowledged the mistake and its consequences as soon as they were aware of it and sought the continuing benefit of the atonement immediately.[43]

In the light of our present bodily reality, we need the merits of Christ's death every moment, and Wesley stresses that the whole basis of our restored relationship is God's grace, and it is never our achievement. This means that we will always need the merits of Christ's death and his intercession for all our shortcomings that inevitably go with bodily life as we currently know it. Wesleyans affirm that weakness of understanding, and a thousand infirmities, remain while we continue to live in this corruptible body, but sin itself need not remain. The highest perfection we can attain while in this present, bodily existence does not exclude ignorance and error, nor countless other limitations of body, mind, and emotions. We do not have perfect knowledge or understanding, so our judgments and subsequent decisions and actions will be faulty and potentially damaging. This is clearly short of the performance that Adam could give prior to the Fall, but the atonement graciously covers this if we confess our fault as soon as the Spirit makes us aware of it.

A sanctified life is essentially the in-dwelling presence of the triune God—Father, Son, and Holy Spirit—and their pure love filling the heart, expelling all that is contrary to God's character. This love is then to be fully and freely returned to God in an ever-deepening relationship that embraces the neighbour and their welfare. This pure love moulds and shapes us into the very image of Christ, despite the current limitations of our bodily existence.

SIN

Numerous Hebrew and Greek words form our theological concept of sin (in English, these include but are not limited to: defiance, offense, violation, transgressions, iniquity, rebellion, and lawlessness). This concept is further expanded when we include the various biblical accounts where a clear act of sin transpires, even when the terminology is not directly used. The story of the Fall in Genesis 3 is a perfect example of this. The one thing that the biblical accounts of sin have in common is that they are ultimately perceived as an offence against God. In the words of King David, "Against you, you alone have I sinned, and done what is evil in your sight" (Psalm 51:4). Sin is defined in relationship to God and God's mission. In a very real way, sin is a breakdown in this primary relationship with God. Our actions will most likely also cause a break down in our relationship with other persons. Yet, they simultaneously negatively impact our relationship with God, since God is love and desires for us to love others as a way of evidencing our love for God (John 13:34-35; Galatians 5:14; 1 John 4:12). From a Wesleyan perspective, willful (conscious and voluntary) sins are a problem because they stunt our relationship with God and others. Willful sin is an intentional move away from love, whereas Christian perfection is a continual, abiding in love (in Christ).

"Love Excluding Sin"

The core of Christian perfection (and salvation as a whole) is "desire" and not intellectual knowledge or actions. We can think things, say things, and do things that might appear to others (and even to ourselves due to the deceitfulness of our hearts) as holy. Nevertheless, if these things flow from a place of selfishness or self-centredness, which is not what the Lord seeks from the children of God, then they are not holy. The love of God is a desire, a passion, that enables our thoughts, words, and deeds to be pleasing in God's sight. The vital quality is a heart that is right toward God (a relationship), seeking only to love, glorify, and enjoy God forever through faith in Jesus Christ. This means that the critical question is what lies behind our outward actions. Do our actions spring from a love for God or not? The Bible (as we saw earlier) clearly refers to the need for both cleansing and purity, and states quite plainly that our hearts are not "naturally" that way. It is only by God's grace that our unclean, impure hearts can become a place fit for the fullness of Christ to dwell.

This raises the question—are our hearts cleansed from sin first and then filled with love, or does the infilling of love cleanse it? Does the sequence even matter? Wesley's preferred picture of the experience of Christian perfection begins with the person's positive desire to be filled with love rather than having sin cleansed away.[44] If we picture our heart as a dirty container that we want to use as a drinking vessel holding pure water, it can be made fit for that purpose in one of two ways. Either it is made clean first and then filled with pure water, or the pure water itself fills the container with such power that all the dirt is washed away, leaving a clean vessel filled with clean water. The potential problem with trying to be clean is that we are never sure when we are "clean enough". Have we missed "a bit of dirt" that will detract from the presence of Christ in our heart?

On the other hand, if the power of divine love is so great that it expels all that is unclean, then the focus shifts: we become more open to this love and leave the outcome of receiving love to its own power. The emphasis is on the positive presence of love in the heart that leaves no room for anything contrary. This keeps the focus on seeking a deeper relationship that is always transformative rather than trying to be in a fit state to receive a blessing. In other words, it is the infilling of love that lies at the heart of the experience, not a requirement for prior cleansing or purification before love can enter. Wesley was not entirely consistent at this point due to his conviction that God could work as God pleased in a person's life. Wesley admitted that speaking of the cleansing as prior to the infilling of love was more useful in certain contexts, particularly when dealing with the issue of sin itself.

Receivable Now by Faith Alone

Wesley held to the understanding that God fitted the conditions required for a relationship with God to the capacities and abilities of God's human creatures. After the Fall, with everyone losing both the capacity and ability to perfectly maintain these requirements, God—in an act of unmerited love—established a new covenant of grace that requires faith alone:

> Exactly as we are justified by faith, so are we sanctified by faith.
> Faith is the condition, and the only condition of sanctification,

exactly as it is of justification. It is the condition: none is sanctified but he that believes; without faith no [one] is sanctified. And it is the only condition: this alone is sufficient for sanctification.[45]

Just as we are born again by grace alone and faith alone, so we are sanctified wholly by grace alone and faith alone. Our life with Christ begins in faith and is maintained in faith, including our entire sanctification. Wesley was keenly aware that we tend to start in faith but then subtly drift towards doing things by our own efforts, self-discipline, self-denial, and a range of spiritual practices. It is not that these things are wrong but that we trust in them for transformation, rather than trusting the Holy Spirit who can work through them. On the other hand, while the experience is receivable by faith alone, it is not a matter of simply waiting passively for God to do the work of grace in the heart. This is why repentance is an essential part of the whole spiritual journey and not simply an initial requirement. Repentance can be thought of as a kind of self-knowledge that, through the work of the Spirit, makes us aware of the need for a deeper work of grace and then invites God to do this work. All the while, we continue to walk in all the light that we currently have, and we are open to receive the grace of entire sanctification as God's gift. It is our confidence in God's love for us (1 John 3:1-3) that enables faith (trust) to arise as a response. We can, by the power of the Spirit, both resist and conquer sin, weakening its hold on us, yet we cannot deliver ourselves from it. This is the work of God and the work of God alone, for God alone can purge us from human selfishness in all its forms and expressions.

Instantaneously

A key point of debate is whether this experience of grace is realized gradually or instantaneously. Attempts have been made to "prove" the point one way or the other from isolated texts of Scripture. Wesleyans, however, affirm the experience and teaching of a long list of witnesses throughout the history of the church who have testified to it being an instantaneous gift. Wesley denied there was a final victory over sin in this life unless and until God worked at a subsequent time to bring about a full deliverance. He believed that this gift of faith was usually given in a moment. Wesley illustrated that a person might be dying for some time, but there is an actual moment of death.[46] We can be dying to sin bit by bit during our Christian journey (the gradual element of our relationship with God), but there must come a moment when it is dead. If we think in terms of heart purity, there must come a "moment" when the heart is pure. The advertising slogan that a product is 99% pure simply means that it is impure. Purity, by its very definition, is 100% or the thing is impure. The heart is either "filled" with love, or it is not. That means there must be a moment when it ceases to be 99% and becomes 100%. This is true relationally. If I am 99% faithful to my spouse, it means I am unfaithful!

If we are trying to deal with something in our life before we ask God for the blessing of perfect love, then we are still seeking to be sanctified by works. If it is entered into by faith, we can ask God to do the work just as we are, and, therefore, to do it now. If the person did not expect an instantaneous change, then Wesley thought it was unlikely that they would ever experience Christian perfection before death. If there is merely a gradual work of God (Wesleyans do not deny that there is a gradual work) then we are unlikely to be delivered from the power of in-being sin this side of death. That does not mean that this moment was necessarily dramatic and obvious. Late in life Wesley wrote to a member of one of the Methodist societies: "Gradual sanctification may increase from the time you [were] justified; but full deliverance from sin, I believe, is always instantaneous—at least I never yet knew an exception".[47] However, he was always open to the Spirit working as the Spirit pleased and would not reduce things to a simple formula or pattern of activity. The grace was God's to give, and God would do so in a manner and time that pleased God.

The Witness of the Spirit to Christian Perfection

Wesley was convinced that it was the common privilege of every Christian to experience the witness of the Holy Spirit to the reality of Christian perfection, just as it was to their new birth. For some, this awareness of the witness of the Spirit is dramatic, and for others, it is almost unnoticed. For some it is quite long-lasting and steady; for others it passes quickly. There is always a danger of wanting a dramatic experience, and without it, feeling that nothing has really changed. Relying on the depth of our feelings leaves us open to the danger of being deceived, confusing those feelings with the reality. This is where we need to balance our "experience" with the clear teaching of the Bible, the long heritage of the church, as well as our personal and community conscience informed and shaped by Scripture.

The experience of entire sanctification must also lead to a depth of personal transformation that can be demonstrated in life—the fruit of the Spirit (Galatians 5:22-23). Both the direct witness of the Spirit and the fruit of the Spirit go together in the life of believers, and it is the presence of the fruit that minimises the chance of us being wrong about the direct witness of the Spirit. We need to keep in balance the evidence of the internal assurance and the outward change to minimise self-delusion. This is why we must faithfully and prayerfully read and reflect on Scripture, read the writings of the Christian community, attend public worship, and seek wisdom from the saints.

SAINTS

In the New Testament, the word translated as "saints" in English is the plural form of the Greek word for "holy" (*hagios*). It could simply be translated as "holy ones". This concept should not be confused with its historical use within the Church. It does not refer to a single person who has been deemed by the church as being particularly holy because of something he or she did while alive. Furthermore, the title of "saint" is not reserved for those who have died. Instead, in the New Testament, "saint" is a title given to every believer in Christ. If we have faith in Christ and are filled with the Holy Spirit, then we are saints. The apostle Paul regularly refers to those in his churches as "saints by calling," even the church in Corinth who was arguably the most un-Christlike group of believers (1 Corinthians 1:2 NASB). As those who are in Christ, our identities include being holy people or saints. This identity is not necessarily tied to our actions, at least not at first. Instead, it speaks more to the new reality we have entered into as the body of Christ. Therefore, we can speak of this type of holiness as initial sanctification. Notice also that when used in this way, it is always plural. In other words, we do not have individual saints, but rather we are saints together as the Church.

The Nature of Christian Perfection Clarified

The relationship between entire sanctification and Christian perfection is often misunderstood, both by critics and supporters. Initial sanctification and entire sanctification are not two different types of holiness. The first danger we face is undervaluing what God did for us at the moment of initial sanctification. At that moment, God changes us from someone whose life is energised by inward sinfulness to someone energised by inward holiness. Our selfish and self-centred love is transformed by the love of God, delivering us from our bondage to sin. In entire sanctification, this divine love fills the heart completely, resulting in a pure heart that is cleansed from all unrighteousness. Until this point, our love was contaminated by our selfishness and self-centredness, supremely loving someone or something in place of God. Even our best efforts to love our neighbour as we should was often hindered by our own desires. When God works this subsequent change, our whole heart becomes consistent with itself, and there is an authentic integrity to every aspect of our life. Such love cannot be content with simply avoiding evil or minimising harm to the neighbour, it is always seeking to do good to all. Entire sanctification is the initial experience of the fullness of the love of God and neighbour and Christian perfection is the life that flows from that moment in an ever-deepening relationship with God and neighbour.

QUESTIONS FOR REFLECTION

1. How would you explain "in-being sin" to a new Christian?

2. In what ways is entire sanctification both a process and a crisis?

3. Can you be entirely sanctified and still have doubts? Why or why not?

4. How is "Christian perfection" related to "entire sanctification", and how would you explain this to someone else?

5. What is the difference between "sin properly so called" and "involuntary transgressions"?

6. How can we affirm entire sanctification in light of perfect love and imperfect bodies?

7. What are "bodily infirmities", and how are they related to sin?

8. What difference does it make if we describe the way of entering into entire sanctification as "love excluding sin" or as "a heart cleansed from sin"?

9. What is the role of faith in entire sanctification?

10. Is the witness of the Spirit to entire sanctification important?

CHAPTER 7

LOVE, RELATIONSHIPS, AND SPIRITUAL FORMATION

Genuine love is transformative. The only way we can experience this kind of transformative love is in our ongoing, moment-by-moment relationship with Christ. In other words, it is not simply a one-time gift that God gives us to possess. Wesley affirmed this understanding in a letter to Joseph Benson: "Christ does not give light to the soul separate from, but in and with, Himself. ... our perfection is not like that of a tree, which flourishes by the sap derived from its own root; but like that of a branch, which, united to the vine, bears fruit, but severed from it is 'dried up and withered'".[48] Therefore, he admonished his people: "let love not visit you as a transient guest, but be the constant ruling temper of your soul".[49] Wesley urged the Methodists: "Let truth and love possess your whole soul. Let them be the springs of all your affections, passions, tempers; the rule of all your thoughts. Let them inspire all your discourse; ... Let all your actions be wrought in love".[50] He believed that "Christian revelation" had clearly demonstrated that "the love of God [was] the true foundation both of the love of our neighbour and all other virtues", and if the love of neighbour did not "spring from the love of God" it was no virtue at all.[51] He believed that "there have been from the beginning two orders of Christians," based on the strenuousness of their pursuit of Christian holiness.[52]

> From long experience and observation I am inclined to think that whoever finds redemption in the blood of Jesus, ... has then the choice of walking in the higher or the lower path. I believe the Holy Spirit at that time sets before him the more excellent way, and incites him to walk therein, to choose the narrowest path in the narrow way, to aspire after the heights and depths of holiness, after the entire image of God. But if he does not accept this offer, he insensibly declines into the lower order of Christians.[53]

A love-based relationship is not then the excuse to disregard the other commandments God had given. Loving God with a whole-hearted devotion implies a total willingness to please him in all that we do, say, and think: "Love rejoices to obey, to do in every point whatever is acceptable to the Beloved. A true lover of God hastens to do his will on earth as it is done in heaven".[54] The true nature of love is displayed in the life, ministry, and sacrificial death of Jesus Christ. Christ's willingness to empty himself, take on human form, and become obedient to death (Philippians 2:5-7) provides us with an example to follow—both in loving others and being obedient to God.

OBEDIENCE

Throughout his earthly ministry, Jesus demonstrated an obedience to the Father. What we often forget is that Jesus's actions were a reflection of the Father's heart. As Jesus often reminded his disciples, those who had seen him had seen the Father (John 14:9). This is significant in terms of defining obedience. Jesus's actions were not motivated by fear or obligation to a higher authority. They were spurred by a shared love within the Godhead for the whole of creation. Each person of the Godhead participated in this shared mission of bringing salvation and restoration to all.

Likewise, our obedience to God must be motivated by love—first, God's love for us, then, our love for God. Jesus said, "If you love me, you will keep my commandments" (John 14:15). This is not a mandate; it is an affirmation of a new reality for those who abide in Christ and are filled with the Holy Spirit. As we obey, we join with God in his mission of bringing salvation and restoration to all. In and through this obedience, we are being made holy.

We have received God's grace so that we can live in grace-enabled obedience throughout our Christian journey. In fact, we cannot remain in this quality of relationship without seeking to deepen and enrich it, and this is why obedience to God's commands remains central to our discipleship. If the essence of Christianity is love and relationship, then that relationship must be cultivated, and this can only happen through a shared life. Amos 3:3 asks the question: "Can two people walk together without agreeing on the direction?" (NLT). This reminds us that if we are to fully and deeply share the journey, we must be open to God's love and be willing participants in God's desires and pleasures. This cannot be other than transformative if we are truly to share life at the deepest and most intimate of levels.

The life of holiness faces many subtle temptations that can quickly lead us into unhealthy attitudes and practices. One danger is to move from a dependent relationship of love to one where we measure the performance of a range of duties. Some of the Pharisees in the Gospels excellent example of this. They wanted to please God, but they subtly went about things the wrong way and from the wrong motives and ultimately fell prey to perfectionism. Perfectionism demands that we never fall short of the artificial standard we impose on ourselves in terms of success in keeping moral standards and spiritual disciplines. Trying to measure up to a standard of perfect performance leads to constant guilt and condemnation when we know we fail, and then redoubling the discipline and the effort to not fail the next time. Ironically, it makes us more self-centred than ever, as we constantly check how we are doing.

Closely tied to this is legalism. Legalism measures our success at performing duties, having good habits, and attending to religious observances. We adopt a standard for each of these and subtly (or sometimes not so subtly) disparage those who do not meet our self-imposed standard. It is true that God is concerned with our habits, lifestyles, and worship, but these are to flow from a heart of love, not be straightjackets to create a holy life. Part of our human nature is the exercise of discernment, but this can so easily slip into judgementalism. We can become preoccupied with both performance and legalism, which often leads to classifying others as being more or less spiritual based on our own categories. We can become increasingly judgemental of others while being gentler on our own faults and failings. Turning holiness into a private and individualistic experience divorced from a social connection or focusing endlessly on how I feel or how I am doing all divide us from the rich experience of God's loving grace.

GRACE

The Greek word *karis* is most often translated as "grace". Nevertheless, this is not a simple concept to define. In Greek, it carries the ideas of and can be translated as "gratitude," "esteem," "charm," "goodwill," "favour," and "gift" (just to name a few). When speaking about God's grace, the last word is especially significant; grace is the gift of God. But what is the gift? Who is the gift given to? And do we need to reciprocate the gift? We often hear people speak about "salvation" as the gift; however, in a very real sense, we can say that God (Father, Son, and Holy Spirit) is the gift. Every action of God toward creation is a gift, and the greatest gift of all is the relationship God invites us into. It is a gift that we neither deserve nor could earn, but one that is freely and continuously offered to us, because God loves us and desires this relationship with us.

Wesleyans believe this gift is offered to all humanity regardless of who they are or what they have done or not done (see John 3:16). Still, God does not force this gift upon us; we have a choice. In terms of reciprocity, God does not require payment for this grace, otherwise it would not be a gift. But "the receipt of this gift is necessarily expressed in gratitude, obedience, and transformed behaviour. This grace is free (unconditional) but not cheap (without expectation or obligation). Those who have received it are to remain within it, live lives altered by new habits, new dispositions, and new practices of grace".[55] In other words, grace should lead to holiness.

If we are to avoid these failings, then we need to avoid the trap of seeing holy living as a performance put on for God (and neighbour). No amount of self-discipline and devotion will ever earn God's favour, focusing on outward words and actions ignores the reality of our motives and attitudes, about which God has much to say. We are called to live in a trusting, open, receptive, and obedient relationship with God, in which God's loving grace enables a holy life. The key element is the quality of the relationship, not the power of the performance. There is an ever-present need to deepen the relationship with God, so that we become mature in Christ: gaining in wisdom, insight, knowledge, and speech. Loving actions do not automatically flow from a loving heart, so we must take seriously the complexities of human life and behaviours.

God alone is able to explore our hidden depths, bring them into the light of God's love, and, with our permission, apply healing and renewal. There is nothing in our life that could possibly cause God to love us less. After all Christ went to the cross for us while we were still his bitter enemy (Romans 5:6-9). This is part of the journey of faith, and to pull back here because we do not want to face the depths of our being is to limit the benefit of God's healing grace. God wants to reorient all our affections, intentions, and motives, and we must not throw away our confidence in the work of the Spirit as God does so. At times our emotional state will be frail, and we will feel abandoned by God. Satan uses this as an opportunity to insinuate we have sinned or to make self-justification and sinful actions attractive. We need to learn to surrender our feelings (and our lack of feelings) to the control of the Holy Spirit, admitting we cannot deal with them and trusting God's grace to keep us in Christ.

Real spiritual maturity comes when we stop trying to hide ourselves from ourselves. When we are truly secure in God's love, we can freely admit our shortcomings and defects rather than try to justify them as "that's just the way I am". This maturity allows God to truly deal with our blind spots and weaknesses. It allows God to bring a true, healing forgiveness for the hurts of the past and enables us to accept responsibility for our own behaviour and attitudes, rather than endlessly blaming others. God can and does bring powerful moments of healing and deliverance, but very often, God does this over time, enabling a genuine growth in holy love. The true test of our love for God is how much we focus on our neighbours and their welfare rather than on our own self-improvement. A holy life is a life that is offered to God as an instrument of grace for a dark and broken world. As John Oswalt reminds us, being holy as God is holy is not a demand but an offer![56]

Our culture so often lets us think that "being" and "doing" are two separate things. We reason that correct behaviour will simply arise from correct belief. We tend to separate "theory" and "practice" and prioritise theory over practice. Thus, a Bible study about love becomes more important than actually loving our difficult neighbour. Such patterns of thought are alien to the biblical and early church world, where human life is more integrated and communal. The New Testament demonstrates how practices like "table fellowship" and hospitality are not simply illustrations of beliefs. The practices generate the realities they are thought to represent and actually restructure relationships and engender transformed patterns of human life.[57] This reminds us of the critical importance of "habituated practice" in the life of holiness, both personally and communally. This was central to Wesley's formative practice for his Methodist people and one that needs to be at the heart of holy living.

Spiritual formation in the Wesleyan framework is fundamentally relational (see companion book in the series: *Embodying a Theology of Ministry and Leadership*[58]). While personal and private spiritual exercises are essential, they cannot replace interaction with the neighbour. Likewise, being open and receptive to the possibility of transformation is not limited to our first conscious contact with God. It is equally true for every step of our journey with God. All of this can be done by the direct work of the Holy Spirit in our heart or by the use of various "means of grace". The means of grace are an essential part of Wesleyan spiritual formation, both personally and corporately. They are defined as "the outward signs, words, or actions ordained of God and appointed to this end, to be the ordinary channels whereby he might convey to us preventing, justifying or sanctifying grace".[59] They are a set of personal and community practices that mediate the transformative power of God's love to us, and without the living presence of the Spirit, they have no benefit at all.

While God can work in any way God pleases, Wesley observed that God most commonly worked through "means", that is, through a specific, intentional source. We can compare this to the need for plants to have water if they are to live and flourish. Rain can fall on an area and water all the plants in that location. However, the rain is not a "means" of delivering water to specific plants. A bucket or a hose is needed to carry the water from a source to the plant that needs water. Neither the bucket nor the hose has any power in themselves to water the plant. They simply carry the water, which is the actual source of refreshment. Wesley affirmed that God could bless people in all sorts of non-specific ways. Still, God could also bless them through specific means—such as reading the Bible and prayer (what Wesley called "works of piety") or acts of service to neighbour and giving to the poor (what Wesley called "works of mercy").

It is important to remember that grace is not given at some moment in the past to act like a "slow-release" medication that works for the rest of our lives. Grace is the living presence of Christ, and we need help to keep the relationship strong moment by moment. Sadly, the means of grace are often forgotten in many Wesleyan-Holiness churches, which instead emphasise revivalism, the direct inspiration of the Holy Spirit, and a slight distrust of structure. This is because these churches and the people in them value personal and corporate freedom and do not want to be bound by formal worship or discipleship practices. However, God's covenant relationship with us is neither one-sided and coercive, nor is it spontaneous. It requires the ongoing, empowering work of the Holy Spirit and our cooperation with that work. No relationship will survive or flourish without intentionality and firm commitment on our part. Habits really matter for spiritual formation. Otherwise, we simply act impulsively or when we feel like it.

We need intentional practices of such things as Bible reading, prayer, worship, helping the neighbour, and other spiritual disciplines that take place within a community with a specific purpose. The purpose is to intentionally challenge the personal and cultural practices that limit our relationships with God and our neighbour. These disciplines are not merely spiritual exercises but acts of resistance to make us more aware of and less formed by our cultural and social expectations. We need to adopt simple, quiet, but powerful habits to reshape our orientation toward the world. Such habits are not divinely implanted at conversion but must be intentionally developed in our lifetime.

The critical issue is how human response relates to God's grace. While our current culture or cultures may not value embedding these practices in concrete forms (liturgical, communal, devotional, etc.), our Wesleyan heritage does value these visible disciplines. By nature, we are self-idolatrous and slaves to the things of this world, and the way of discipline can wean us from our worldly attachments and free us for God's service. The promise of God for deliverance from remaining sin and empowering for a life of holy love requires an intentional obedience, not careless indifference or lazy activity. It is true that we receive this gift by simple faith, but God does not and will not give that faith unless we seek it with all diligence in the way God has ordained. The means of grace are important because of our human weakness.

DISCIPLESHIP

The Greek word *mathētēs*, usually translated as "disciple" in English, refers to a pupil who is being trained or instructed by a teacher. Jesus had many disciples, most of whom not only followed his teachings but also literally followed him. This was part of the typical Jewish rabbi (teacher)-student relationship. Students were expected to go and do everything their rabbi went and did. By listening and watching, they learned both formally and informally. Furthermore, they discovered how to apply everything they were learning. Ultimately, many Jewish disciples went on to become rabbis and have disciples of their own.

In the same way, Jesus commissioned his disciples to "make disciples of all nations" (Matthew 28:19). From a Christian perspective, "Discipleship is the means by which those who are disciples of Christ help make other disciples of Christ. ... a person must be a disciple of Christ in order to do Christlike discipleship. The reality is that we reproduce ourselves in the discipleship process".[60] As Paul wrote, "Follow my example, as I follow the example of Christ" (1 Corinthians 11:1, NIV). It is important that our discipleship is both taught and caught. In other words, we must live out our faith and intentionally invite others to do as we are doing. Like Jesus did with his disciples, we must lovingly challenge them to grow, free them to be themselves, empower them to do ministry, and call them to make disciples of others.

In terms of holiness, discipleship is part of being transformed and living out our holiness. As disciples of Christ, we are called to grow in our relationship with God and others. In the discipleship process we intentionally enter into relationships that keep us accountable and help facilitate such growth. It should also be stressed that discipleship is about relationship. It is not about a list of things to do or not do or about a hoop to jump through. Genuine discipleship only takes place in community and requires openness to others in order to truly flourish in our relationship with God.

Discipleship is not simply about doing certain actions out of duty or obligation. It increases our receptivity to God's love poured into our hearts by the Holy Spirit, increases our capacity to receive and share the love God and neighbour, and increases our inclination to exercise that love in practical ways. The life of faith is a dynamic life; such development requires active involvement in a community of faith, personal and community discipline, and an intense desire for an ever-increasing depth of personal and corporate transformation. It involves every aspect and every moment of daily life—not just what happens in church, a Bible study, or a prayer meeting. The habits that we need to form include such elements as self-denial, prayer, fasting, the Lord's Supper, community worship, private devotions, scripture reading, small groups, and seeking the welfare of the neighbour through compassionate ministry. However, the means cannot be substituted for our actual relationship with God nor become an end in themselves. Of these habits, the life of the Christian "neighbour" can often have the greatest impact. Our personal devotional life is very important, but the greatest transformation comes through the challenges we face in developing God-honouring relationships. If we do not remain open to the possibilities of a deeper connection, we will be tempted to settle for our current experience.

The Christian life is always grounded in faith, and if our relationship with God is to flourish, we must continue to trust God. Because love, trust, and relationships are interlinked and interdependent, the depth of love and trust determines the depth and strength of the relationship—whether with God or with our neighbour. It is very easy to say we love someone who is at a distance; the real test is what happens when we meet face to face. We can "love" the poor and dispossessed overseas quite easily, but what happens when we meet them on the street or at our local church? We can easily talk about "loving" those who hold different opinions about doctrine, conduct, or worship practices, as long as they attend another church. What happens when they become members of our church? Very few Christians admit to racial, cultural, or lifestyle prejudice. It is only when we are confronted by the physical presence of the "other" that we become aware of all the negative feelings they stir up and expose. Sometimes it is much easier to allow the church rules and regulations to replace love and friendship. Our struggles to do this because of prejudice, misunderstanding, and faulty judgement are used by the Spirit to uncover the true state of our heart and just how passionate we really are about loving God and our neighbour. Obedience flows from love of God in the heart by the Spirit, and it is not tied to a feeling of love (or any other emotion). We are to obey even if no positive feelings motivate or accompany the decision. There will be many occasions when we do not "feel" like helping another or when we do not emotionally connect with a person. However, we are still to feed the hungry, give water to the thirsty, clothe the naked, visit the sick and imprisoned—for love's sake alone.

The call is always to trust the God of our experience rather than trust our experience of God. This is especially true for those of us who have the types of personality and temperament that traditionally have not been associated with being "holy". Too often we have identified placidity as the ideal temperament, though some overvalue excitability and high emotion. We need to realise there is no such thing as a "Christlike" temperament or personality trait. Instead, the various temperaments can be expressed in un-Christlike or Christlike ways. We need to trust God with our personality and temperament, allowing the Holy Spirit to refine and mould us in ways that will enhance our flourishing. Given our human frailty and emotional instability, we do not always "feel" loved or accepted. In such instances, it is very easy to believe God has abandoned us and that we are no longer God's children. It is so important that we do not confuse depression (brought on by such things as tiredness, illness, and frailty) with spiritual darkness. Our emotional state is not an infallible guide to our spiritual state (both positively and negatively—feelings of euphoria are no more indicative of holiness than feelings of depression are of sin). Christians are able to live in the reality of perfect love while battling depression and grief, since emotion can neither create nor destroy the work of God in the heart.

If we are to have strong, healthy relationships that glorify God and form us into Christ's likeness, we will need to embrace God's grace, wisdom, discernment, and guidance. We must be receptive to the work of the Holy Spirit through the body of Christ and the wider community. We must recognise that we are all unique and that each particular situation and particular practice will always need the help of the Spirit, both personally and communally. We discern this best by looking to Scripture and the Christian community, that is to say the public, long-time interpretation, application, and demonstration of the Scriptures. This is where the group structures used by Wesley are so important. In Wesley's day, regular gatherings for public worship nourished the spiritual life of the Methodists. However, they (and we) needed a deep, Christian fellowship in smaller groups to form their lives, both personal and communal. In smaller groups, we are able to offer encouragement to one another, examine together the teachings of Jesus and how they might be applied, watch over one another in love, pray for each other and help each other in practical ways. Wesley also saw the immense value in small, intimate groups (that he called "bands") of six to eight people to help develop a life of Christian holiness. These voluntary groups were for those who were serious about Christian perfection. They were highly confessional in nature, with each member being open and vulnerable through confessing their sins and their struggles in a setting of mutual forgiveness and love. These groups had a more demanding discipline as they encouraged one another to "carefully" avoid evil, "zealously" do good works, and "constantly" observe the practices of both their personal spiritual life and that of their local church.

However, nothing ultimately substitutes for close friendships, especially those that occur face to face. Contact by phone, internet, email, text, and video are all wonderful helps, but none are substitutes for physical presence. We need to reinvigorate our "works of mercy" (active service to help the neighbour) in personal and community practice, for the sake of love alone. It is by a physical, shared relationship, walking and talking together, sharing experiences and meals together, and serving together that enables God to work in ways and at depths that will not happen otherwise. This means that we must be actively involved in reaching out to new people, genuinely offering them hospitality, and cultivating relationships without any hidden agenda. That is to say, we offer hospitality without seeking to make them Christian. It means that within the church, we must be committed to all who form part of the community and actively seek ways to nourish the relationship by serving them in love. It is precisely the struggles to enter, maintain, and develop a variety of relationships that enables the Holy Spirit to transform at the deepest levels. Christian holiness is essentially pure love filling our hearts, expelling all that is contrary to God's nature. This love is fully and freely returned in an ever-deepening fellowship that fully participates in the life of the triune God. Such a love equally embraces and shares in the life of the neighbour as an essential companion on the journey. God's love expressed in these relationships forms us into the very image of Christ, so that we are consequently both holy and happy in fulfilling our God-given purpose, in spite of the current limitations of our bodily existence.

QUESTIONS FOR REFLECTION

1. How does perfect love relate to keeping the other commandments?

2. What are some of the major temptations faced by those who would claim to be entirely sanctified?

3. What are "means of grace", and why are they important in spiritual formation?

4. Why is it so important to be part of a Christian community as we seek to mature in Christ?

CHAPTER 8

CONCLUSION

We have seen how Wesley's understanding of salvation rested on God's love for humanity and humanity's response to that love. Unlike our Calvinist brothers and sisters, Wesley believed that a loving God accommodates our present bodily existence and what is now possible for us due to the consequences of sin. The interdependent relationship of love and freedom leads Wesley to conclude that guilt and shame are intimately linked with our intentions and willful choices. Consequently, God makes a gracious allowance for the present limitations of our understanding, will, reason, and conscience and the impact these have on our performance. God still has an absolute requirement for us, but it is for love and relationships, not flawless obedience to the law.

The evidence of having received God's love lies primarily in the heart, in terms of personal trust, rather than outward obedience; Christian perfection is to love God with our whole being and our neighbour as ourselves. In this framework, sin is, strictly speaking, a voluntary (willful) breach of the law of love. Breakdowns in relationships may occur without deliberate intent. Thus, they are, strictly speaking, an infirmity that does not bring condemnation. Even so, all such imperfections need the atoning work of Christ, and a grace-enabled, wholehearted endeavour to do better in the future. For Wesley, such a perfection is possible by divine grace and human openness, receptivity, and ever-deeper trust. For Calvinist Christians, the only perfection acceptable before God is a

79

perfected perfection—a flawless performance of every requirement of the law. For Wesley, the perfection acceptable before God is a perfecting perfection[61] —a dynamic relationship of love that shows itself in character transformation and service to God and neighbour. In the end, it comes down to a decision about the essential nature of our life with God— performance (Calvinist) or passion (Wesley)? Does God require the same level of performance now as God did in the original creation, or does God make an allowance for the reality of present bodily existence? This is the crucial point on which Wesley's whole claim to Christian perfection as a reality in this life stands or falls.

The Church of the Nazarene believes (as do many other denominations that trace their roots to Wesley and early Methodism) that the teaching and ministry of John Wesley is not simply an interesting part of the history of the Church. Nor are they something that only dealt with the conditions of his own time and place but have no relevance for people today from many different nations and cultures. What Wesley rediscovered from his reading of Scripture and the works of the great saints of the Church, as well as the life of his own Methodist people, is essential to the Christian faith for all peoples, at all times, and in every place. The goal of this short text is not to teach some doctrinal truths from long ago. Rather, it is to challenge each of us to know and serve the same Lord Jesus through a deep, grace-enabled love that will impact our local community in such a way that the life of all Christ-followers, their families and their friends are transformed by love and serve God in an ever-increasing measure.

May we find ourselves able to say this prayer (based on the hymn "O Thou Who Camest from Above" by Charles Wesley).[62]

Prayer

Lord Jesus Christ, you came down to earth from heaven to bring the holy fire of divine love that would cleanse us from our sin.

Let my broken, self-centred heart be set ablaze with your holy love.

*May it burn brightly for your glory with
a flame that nothing can put out.*

*May I freely return this love to you in hum-
ble prayer and impassioned praise.*

*Lord Jesus, confirm my heart's desire to
work, and speak, and think for you.*

*By your mercies, enable me to protect this holy fire even
as you continually refresh this gracious gift in me.*

Let me be ready to do all of your perfect will.

*May all my acts of faith and love be repeated till death shall
bring to a close all of your endless mercies that I receive each day,*

And make my living sacrifice complete.

Amen

QUESTIONS FOR REFLECTION

1. What are the key lessons you have learned from your study?

2. How would you make use of this information in helping others to experience and live a holy life?

APPENDIX

The Foreword of the current *Church of the Nazarene Manual* states: "The primary objective of the Church of the Nazarene is to advance God's kingdom by the preservation and propagation of Christian holiness as set forth in the Scriptures". Additionally, the historical statement within the *Manual* reminds us that this is in full harmony with the teaching of the whole church, though it does find its critical insight from the ministry of John and Charles Wesley in the 18th century. Our Article of Faith dealing with this subject is Article 10.

X. Christian Holiness and Entire Sanctification

10. We believe that sanctification is the work of God which transforms believers into the likeness of Christ. It is wrought by God's grace through the Holy Spirit in initial sanctification, or regeneration (simultaneous with justification), entire sanctification, and the continued perfecting work of the Holy Spirit culminating in glorification. In glorification we are fully conformed to the image of the Son.

We believe that entire sanctification is that act of God, subsequent to regeneration, by which believers are made free from original sin, or depravity, and brought into a state of entire devotement to God, and the holy obedience of love made perfect.

It is wrought by the baptism with or infilling of the Holy Spirit, and comprehends in one experience the cleansing of the heart from sin and the abiding, indwelling presence of the Holy Spirit, empowering the believer for life and service. Entire sanctification is provided by the blood of Jesus, is wrought instantaneously by grace through faith, preceded by entire consecration; and to this work and state of grace the Holy Spirit bears witness.

This experience is also known by various terms representing its different phases, such as "Christian perfection," "perfect love," "heart unity," "the baptism with or infilling of the Holy Spirit," "the fullness of the blessing," and "Christian holiness".

10.1. We believe that there is a marked distinction between a pure heart and a mature character. The former is obtained in an instant, the result of entire sanctification; the latter is the result of growth in grace.

We believe that the grace of entire sanctification includes the divine impulse to grow in grace as a Christlike disciple. However, this impulse must be consciously nurtured, and careful attention given to the requisites and processes of spiritual development and improvement in Christlikeness of character and personality. Without such purposeful endeavour, one's witness may be impaired and the grace itself frustrated and ultimately lost.

Participating in the means of grace, especially the fellowship, disciplines, and sacraments of the Church, believers grow in grace and in wholehearted love to God and neighbour.

(Jeremiah 31:31-34; Ezekiel 36:25-27; Malachi 3:2-3; Matthew 3:11-12; Luke 3:16-17; John 7:37-39; 14:15-23; 17:6-20; Acts 1:5; 2:1-4; 15:8-9; Romans 6:11-13, 19; 8:1-4, 8-14; 12:1-2; 2 Corinthians 6:14–7:1; Galatians 2:20; 5:16-25; Ephesians 3:14-21; 5:17-18, 25-27; Philippians 3:10-15; Colossians 3:1-17; 1 Thessalonians 5:23-24; Hebrews 4:9-11; 10:10-17; 12:1-2; 13:12; 1 John 1:7, 9) ("Christian perfection," "perfect love": Deuteronomy 30:6; Matthew 5:43-48; 22:37-40; Romans 12:9-21; 13:8-10; 1 Corinthians 13; Philippians 3:10-15; Hebrews 6:1; 1 John 4:17-18 "Heart purity": Matthew 5:8; Acts 15:8-9; 1 Peter 1:22; 1 John 3:3 "Baptism with the Holy Spirit": Jeremiah 31:31-34; Ezekiel 36:25-27; Malachi 3:2-3; Matthew 3:11-12; Luke 3:16-17; Acts 1:5; 2:1-4; 15:8-9 "Fullness of the blessing": Romans 15:29 "Christian holiness": Matthew 5:1–7:29; John 15:1-11; Romans 12:1–15:3; 2 Corinthians 7:1; Ephesians 4:17-5:20; Philippians 1:9-11; 3:12-15; Colossians 2:20–3:17; 1 Thessalonians 3:13; 4:7-8; 5:23; 2 Timothy 2:19-22; Hebrews 10:19-25; 12:14; 13:20-21; 1 Peter 1:15-16; 2 Peter 1:1-11; 3:18; Jude 20-21)[64]

NOTES

1. John Wesley, *The Letters of the Rev. John Wesley,* 8 Volumes (Telford, London: Epworth Press, 1931), 8:238; henceforth referred to as *Letters* (Telford).

2. Floyd T. Cunningham, *Expressing a Nazarene Identity, Frameworks for Lay Leadership Series,* edited by Rob A. Fringer (Lenexa, KS: Global Nazarene Publications, 2018).

3. "Although we desire to be happy, that is not truly possible until after death because only then can we be delivered from all care, affliction, danger, and especially from all sin." John Wesley, *The Bicentennial Edition of the Works of John Wesley,* edited by Frank Baker et al. (Nashville, TN: Abingdon, 1984ff), 4:206; henceforth referred to as *Works.*

4. David B. McEwan, *Exploring a Wesleyan Theology, Frameworks for Lay Leadership Series,* edited by Rob A. Fringer (Lenexa, KS: Global Nazarene Publications, 2017).

5. Rob A. Fringer, *Engaging the Story of God, Frameworks for Lay Leadership Series,* edited by Rob A. Fringer (Lenexa, KS: Global Nazarene Publications, 2018).

6. William M. Greathouse and H. Ray Dunning, *An Introduction to Wesleyan Theology* (Kansas City, MO: Beacon Hill, 1989), 24.

7. All Scripture quotations are from the NRSV unless otherwise noted.

8. Kent Brower, *Holiness in the Gospels* (Kansas City: Beacon Hill, 2005), 24.

9. Levites: Leviticus 21; Numbers 3:5-13; 2 Chronicles 23:6; prophets: 2 Kings 4:9; Jeremiah 1:5; Nazirite vow: Numbers 6:1-21; Israelites: Deuteronomy 7:6; 14:2.

10. See Gerhard von Rad, *Holy War in Ancient Israel,* translated and edited by Marva Dawn (Grand Rapids: Eerdmans, 1991).

11. Gordon J. Thomas, "A Holy God among a Holy People in a Holy Place: The Enduring Eschatological Hope," pages 53-69 in *Eschatology in Bible & Theology: Evangelical Essays at the Dawn of a New Millennium* (Downers Grove, InterVarsity, 1997), 58.

12. David P. Wright, "Holiness, Old Testament," Pages 237-249 in *Anchor Bible Dictionary: Volume 3,* edited by David N. Freedman et al. (New York: Doubleday, 1992), 246.

13. These words by Brower, *Holiness in the Gospels,* capture this well: "For Jesus, holiness is contagious, outgoing, embracing, and joyous. It transforms and brings reconciliation. It extends compassion to the marginalized so that they are brought into the circle of those who do the will of God. This holiness is

a dynamic power emanating from the source of holiness, the Holy One. It is stronger than any acquired impurity" (129).

14. *Works* 2:179-80.

15. *Works* 3:189; quoted from Augustine, Confessions, 1.1.1.

16. *Works* 3:355-56.

17. *Works*, 3:189.

18. *Works*, 3:533-34. See also *Works*, 21:477-79. Wesley came to the conclusion that to preach in a place without forming a Society was to effectively condemn the new Christians to an eventual loss of faith; see *Works*, 21:424-25.

19. Richard Giesken, *Entering the Mission of God, Frameworks for Lay Leadership Series,* edited by Rob A. Fringer (Lenexa, KS: Global Nazarene Publications, 2018).

20. John Goldingay, *Old Testament Theology: Volume 2,* Israel's Faith (Downers Grove: IVP Academic, 2006), 201.

21. Rob A. Fringer, "Regeneration/Rebirth," pages 331-333 in *Global Wesleyan Encyclopedia of Biblical Theology,* edited by Robert Branson (Kansas City, MO: Foundry, 2020), 332.

22. See *Works*, 1:264, 317-19; 19:153-59.

23. E.g., Deuteronomy 30:6; Psalm 130:8; Ezekiel 36:25-29; Matthew 5:48; Romans 8:3-4; 2 Corinthians 7:1; Ephesians 3:14-19; 5:25-28; 1 Thessalonians 5:23; 1 John 3:8-9

24. E.g., Romans 6:12-14; Titus 2:11-14; Luke 1:69-75

25. *Works*, 19: 294-96.

26. John Wesley, *The works of John Wesley: Volume 11,* edited by Thomas Jackson (London: Wesleyan Methodist Bookroom, 1872), 11:393; henceforth referred to as *Works* (Jackson).

27. *Works*, 2:119-20.

28. *Works*, 2:120-21.

29. Since Christ took on human flesh, it is likely that he would have had some physical defects or blemishes. Therefore, we cannot take this statement of absolute perfection too far. Using Wesley's definitions, we could say that Christ was without sin but not without human infirmities.

30. See Outler's introduction in *Works,* 4:200-02.

31. *Works*, 2:194.

32. *Works* 11:339–40.

33. *Works* 9:409.

34. *Letters* (Telford) 4:10.

35. *Works*, 3:73. See also *Works*, 2:405-06, 74, 81-82; 3:159-62.

36. *Works*, 1:241.

37. *Works*, 1:242-43.

38. *Works* 3:179. Emphasis ours.

39. *Works* (Jackson), 11:414-15.

40. *Works* (Jackson), 11:416.

41. *Works* (Jackson), 11:417-18.

42. *Letters* (Telford), 3:168.

43. *Works* (Jackson), 11:419.

44. *Works* (Jackson), 8:284.

45. *Works*, 2:163-64.

46. *Works* (Jackson), 11:402.

47. *Letters* (Telford), 8:190.

48. *Letters* (Telford) 5:204.

49. *Letters* (Telford) 5:422.

50. *Letters* (Telford) 5:426.

51. *Letters* (Telford) 5:279-80. See also *Letters* (Telford) 5:263-77, 306, 522-28.

52. *Letters* (Telford) 5:265.

53. *Letters* (Telford) 5:266.

54. *Works* (Jackson), 11:280.

55. John M. G. Barclay, *Paul & the Power of Grace* (Grand Rapids: Eerdmans, 2020), 149.

56. John Oswalt, *Called to Be Holy: A Biblical Perspective* (Nappanee, IN: Evangel Publishing House, 1999).

57. Joel B. Green, "Embodying the Gospel: Two Exemplary Practices," *Journal of Spiritual Formation & Soul Care* 7:1 (2014), 11-21.

58. Bruce G. Allder, *Embodying a Theology of Ministry and Leadership, Frameworks for Lay Leadership Series,* edited by Rob A. Fringer (Lenexa, KS: Global Nazarene Publications, 2018).

59. *Works,* 1:378-97.

60. This statement has been taken from the Nazarene Asia-Pacific Regional Discipleship Model. Found here: https://asiapacificnazarene.org/wp-content/

uploads/2021/09/Asia-Pacific-Regional-Discipleship-Model-and-Explanation.
pdf.

61. T. A. Nobel, *Holy Trinity: Holy People: The Historic Doctrine of Christian Perfecting* (Eugene, OR: Cascade, 2013).

62. Charles Wesley (1762), 57: https://divinity.duke.edu/sites/divinity.duke.edu/
files/documents/cswt/63_Scripture_Hymns_%281762%29_Vol_1.pdf.

63. *Manual of the Church of the Nazarene, 2017-2021,* edited by Dean Blevins et al. (Kansas City: Nazarene Publishing House, 2017), 5.

64. *Manual,* 2017-2021, 31-32.

CPSIA information can be obtained
at www.ICGtesting.com
Printed in the USA
LVHW030047140222
711064LV00007B/469

9 781563 449505